# INDUSTRY
# IN AFRICA

# INDUSTRY
# IN AFRICA

## A. F. EWING

*With a Foreword by Robert Gardiner*

LONDON
OXFORD UNIVERSITY PRESS
NEW YORK   IBADAN   NAIROBI
1968

*Oxford University Press, Ely House, London W.1*

GLASGOW NEW YORK TORONTO MELBOURNE WELLINGTON
CAPE TOWN SALISBURY IBADAN NAIROBI LUSAKA ADDIS ABABA
BOMBAY CALCUTTA MADRAS KARACHI LAHORE DACCA
KUALA LUMPUR HONG KONG TOKYO

*Printed in Great Britain by*
*Richard Clay (The Chaucer Press) Ltd*
*Bungay, Suffolk*

To my Father

# CONTENTS

## MAPS

# TABLES

# CHART

# FOREWORD

## By ROBERT GARDINER

*Executive Secretary, United Nations Economic Commission for Africa*

In this book Mr. A. F. Ewing discusses in a simple style but with professional competence the problems of industry in Africa. The approach is sympathetic, constructive, and realistic. Eschewing terminological jargon as far as possible, but adhering to a scientific and objective analysis, Mr. Ewing has brought to bear on the subject of African industrialization the thinking developed over a period of five years during which he has been associated with the Economic Commission for Africa. Its primary appeal is to policy-makers interested in the rapid industrial development of this continent. It should also interest serious students of African affairs.

Without overburdening his narrative and analysis with masses of data, the author brings out the salient features of the existing industrial structures of the different African countries. He emphasizes the point that what is required for a rapid transformation of the present economic condition is not industry of any kind but industries which would bring about a structural change. The scope for industries based on import substitution is naturally limited. Intermediate and capital-goods industries have to be developed in order to change the existing structure of the economies and to provide a powerful impetus for rapid all-round economic growth. This view does not belittle the scope for consumer-goods industries and small-scale industries in the context of the present African situation but provides a perspective for future planning which is of vital significance.

If intermediate and capital-goods industries are essential for a breakthrough towards high and accelerated rates of growth, the multi-national and sub-regional approach to economic planning and development advocated by the Economic Commission for Africa appears to be the only logical approach. By and large these industries are capital-intensive and they involve modern and developing technologies. For them the optimum size of output for economic operations is far in excess of what could be absorbed singly by a number of the African countries. From the point of view of the availability of raw materials and power also it is advantageous for groups of countries to come together and promote these industries jointly. Mr. Ewing has reiterated the case for multi-national and sub-regional co-operation in building intermediate and capital-goods industries using both logic and concrete examples. The urgency of joint effort in this field is gradually being appreciated and it is a happy augury that first steps in the direction of setting up an Economic Community for West Africa were taken at the sub-regional meeting of the ECA held at Accra. Since then an agreement has been signed to establish an Economic Community for East Africa.

While advocating a healthy multi-national and sub-regional approach to industrial development, Mr. Ewing has attempted to indicate in broad terms the prospects for different industries in Africa over the next thirty-five to forty years, i.e. until the end of the century. They are more in the nature of informed guesstimates than statistical projections, but against the framework of economic development for the entire continent which he outlines they are interesting. In a way they constitute a perspective plan for the industrialization of Africa which should stimulate further thinking and effort in the right direction. It may be mentioned that the 'industrial perspectives' presented by Mr. Ewing, though seemingly ambitious, are not unrealistic. Given the variety of raw materials and their quality and the potential resources of energy and power with which the continent is endowed, there is no reason why the present level of development in Western Europe should not be attained by Africa by the beginning of the next century. What is needed is well-organized effort.

Viewing the problems of industry in Africa with robust optimism, Mr. Ewing is careful to enumerate the various prerequisites without which the perspectives he has outlined would be difficult to attain. Science, technology, education, manpower planning and training, energy, and transport are some of the prerequisites specially mentioned. Similarly, he suggests that the bulk of finance required to support a programme for the construction of intermediate and capital-goods industries would have to be found from within the continent and could be found. He, however, lays special emphasis, and rightly so, on the human factor, 'the realization that in the last analysis it is people who determine any kind of development'. Publication of Mr. Ewing's *Industry in Africa* at a time when the strategy for African economic development is still in the process of formulation is opportune and should help the process.

# PREFATORY NOTE

The underlying thesis of this book is that industry is the main lever of African development. Yet industry cannot be developed in isolation from the other key sectors of the economy. The experience of the writer, working in the United Nations Economic Commission for Africa in the last five or six years, has shown the difficulty of defining the proper place of industry in the whole complex of development and, beyond this, how many different factors go into the making of an industrial development strategy which is likely to be meaningful in practice. Some consideration is given to the theoretical aspects of the problem, but the main contribution attempted is in the nature of a synthesis, though necessarily a provisional one. It is hoped that the book may be of interest to those concerned with African development problems, particularly policy-makers and their advisers, not only the present generation but perhaps even more the next. It may also be useful to those interested in industrial investment, particularly if it succeeds in directing their attention to the detailed sources which have been drawn upon, especially the rich documentation prepared by the ECA and the stimulus this should provide for more detailed pre-investment studies.

The first chapter considers the role of industrial development, starting from the principal economic trends in Africa since the Second World War; the nature and limitations of Africa's reliance on exports of mining and agricultural products, and world market prospects in these areas; the complementarity of industry and agriculture; import substitution and its limitations; the need to develop high productivity sectors; the contribution of industry to changing the structure of an economy; the way in which growth both requires and makes possible capital formation; and hence the case for industrialization, which in an African context is primarily the development of industry for Africa's own markets. Economies of scale and international specialization are examined, together with external economies and linkage effects and thus the underlying need for the grouping of countries.

The second chapter shows briefly the present pattern of industry in Africa, how it has evolved in recent years, and the immediate objectives of industrial development of African countries. Although statistical information is defective, many factual data are available. No attempt is made at a comprehensive description, and a selective approach is adopted.

The third chapter discusses briefly the experience of other selected developing countries in prompting industrial development.

The fourth chapter discusses the prospects for industrial growth in Africa. Hypotheses for 1975–80 and some broad perspectives of what might be achieved by the end of this century are then set out. Serious projections are not attempted. The experience of the first half of the 1960s, in fact the first half of the 'UN Development Decade', has not been particularly encouraging. Most African plans are still in a rudimentary state and, as will be shown, the institutional and social framework for rapid industrial development has still to be established. Nevertheless, bold long-run perspectives remain valid and necessary. The ECA has worked out such perspectives in some detail, but in this study it is sufficient to adopt an illustrative approach.

The fifth chapter discusses international trade and the grouping of African countries; the prospects for export of industrial products outside Africa; intra-African trade; the relation between industrial integration and integration generally; the common market problem; the lessons to be learned from other parts of the world; the prospects in the four African sub-regions and later in Africa as a whole.

The sixth chapter is concerned with the role of capital, with emphasis on the scope for generating higher rates of domestic saving, and then on problems of foreign capital aid.

The seventh chapter considers briefly infrastructural problems: education and manpower, the discovery of raw materials, energy and transport.

The eighth chapter examines the instruments of industrial development, a subject which has tended to be neglected in Africa.

The ninth and final chapter sets out some brief conclusions.

South Africa is excluded except from time to time for comparative purposes.

The origins of this book lie in part in lectures or papers I have given to discussion groups and seminars, and also in the work of the ECA, to which I have contributed. I have therefore been able to draw heavily on the works and ideas of colleagues too numerous to mention by name. I owe a major intellectual debt to the 'modern' writers on economic development, above all Gunnar Myrdal, my first chief in the United Nations; Destanne de Bernis, Surendra Patel, Dudley Seers, and Hans Singer. I would also like to mention three of my present colleagues: my present chief, Robert Gardiner, whose impatience with under-development and whose immense feeling for the practical have been a major stimulus; and my two successors responsible for the ECA's work in industry, transport, and natural resources, Bax Nomvete and Godfrey Lardner.

The first draft of this book was completed in August 1966, and though in the main revisions, completed at the end of 1966, every effort has been made to bring the material up to date, it should be recognized that this is by no means easy when events are changing fast and the literature is growing so rapidly. Some footnotes relate to information which became available in 1967 at the final stage of preparing this work for the press.

I would like to express my gratitude to the following who have been good enough to comment on the first draft: Samir Amin, Bernard Chidzero, Fred Clairmonte, Jack Dalton, Gerard Dekker, Maurice Dobb, James Ewing, Jean-Louis Lacroix, Alemayu Makonnen, Marc Nerfin, Surendra Patel, Robert Robson, and Hans Singer; and to Max de Henseler for cartographic help.

I owe a debt to Yeworkwoha Mulugeta for typing assistance and an even greater debt to Betty Blackburn, not only for typing but for systematic editorial work (linked with determined encouragement) at every stage in the preparation of this book. I also owe a great deal to the Oxford University Press for their encouragement and the penetrating comments of their readers. Last but not least, I should like to thank David Kimble for compelling me to write this book and introducing me to my publisher.

Needless to say, I alone am responsible for the facts presented, the analysis, and the conclusions drawn, which are not necessarily those of the United Nations Secretariat.

*Kinshasa, 31 December 1966*                    A. F. EWING

The difficulty lies, not in the new ideas, but in escaping from the old ones, which ramify, for those brought up as most of us have been, into every corner of our minds. The ideas of economists and political philosophers, both when they are right and when they are wrong, are more powerful than is commonly understood. Indeed, the world is ruled by little else. Practical men, who believe themselves to be quite exempt from any intellectual influences, are usually the slaves of some defunct economist. Madmen in authority, who hear voices in the air, are distilling their frenzy from some academic scribbler of a few years back. I am sure that the power of vested interests is vastly exaggerated compared with the gradual encroachment of ideas. Not, indeed, immediately, but after a certain interval; for in the field of economic and political philosophy there are not many who are influenced by new theories after they are twenty-five or thirty years of age, so that the ideas which civil servants and politicians and even agitators apply to current events are not likely to be the newest. But, soon or late, it is ideas, not vested interests, which are dangerous for good or evil.

J. M. KEYNES

# CHAPTER I

# THE ROLE OF INDUSTRY IN DEVELOPMENT

It is no longer necessary to argue the case for industrialization as an essential part of the development process. But there are still a number of controversial questions, and therefore in this first chapter the approach adopted throughout this book, the strategy of development and of industrialization itself, is set out briefly. The basic economic reasons for industrialization are given; the relations between industry and agriculture are discussed; import substitution and its limitations are considered. The typical pattern of industrial growth is shown and thus the need to produce intermediate and capital goods at an early stage. Since most African markets are small and economies of scale of crucial importance, this requires the grouping of African economies. External economies and linkage effects cannot be realized within small markets and this is another reason for joint programmes.

In the initial stages of economic development the generator is export of raw materials: agricultural, mining, or petroleum. Normally there is dependence on a limited range of commodities, perhaps only one. Import substitution is limited, since the economy is normally dominated by a metropolitan power. Export markets for raw materials, with limited exceptions, grow relatively slowly owing to relative income elasticities of demand. It has been calculated that a 1 per cent increase in the per capita income of an industrialized country increases the demand for food and raw materials by only 0·6 per cent, but that the same increase in per capita income in a country importing manufactured articles corresponds to an increase of 1·8 per cent in the demand for imports. Although the statistical evidence has been disputed, it is also argued that, superimposed on this basic trend, there has been a tendency, at least since the Second World War, for the terms of trade to move against under-developed countries. If this is true, it by no means follows that the trend will continue. It is relative income elasticities, rather than relative price movements, which are fundamental.

This brief picture of the nature and major problems of an economy in the early stages of development is a general one which applies with particular force to Africa, and there is no need to assemble here the detailed evidence.[1*]

There are no reasons based on either principle or experience which suggest that the future prospects for the export of raw materials are likely to be better than in the past. It has been calculated by the FAO that (taking 1957–59 as 100) the index of the projected volume of net imports of selected agricultural commodities by 1970 is as follows (the importers covered are all high income countries plus the Sino-Soviet area):[2]

| | |
|---|---|
| Sugar | 142–143 |
| Oils | 100–100 |
| Coffee | 138–149 |
| Cocoa | 150–158 |
| Tea | 106–115 |
| Cotton wool and jute | 100–127 |
| Rubber | 111–141 |
| All listed commodities plus citrus fruits | 123–137 |

The largest increases are in cocoa, coffee, tropical wood (not in the figures above), and to a lesser extent rubber. Net imports into Western Europe would increase at 1·5 per cent a year, with a somewhat smaller increase in North America, a larger figure in Japan, and the largest increase of all in the Sino-Soviet area.

Taking all high income areas together plus the centrally planned economies, the highest rate of increase that can be expected is of the order of 2·5 per cent per annum approximately, or perhaps slightly less than the projected rate of population increase.[3]

A more optimistic view sometimes taken, in the light of the official statements made by the USSR and other Eastern European countries at the World Trade Conference held in Geneva in 1964, is that there is every reason to expect that the future import policies of these countries will somewhat improve the prospects of the exporters of agricultural raw materials. Yet there is no evidence to suggest so radical a transformation of the situation as to encourage African countries to remain in their present state of dependence.

* Notes and references to sources will be found at the end of each chapter.

The prospects for some mining products and petroleum are naturally better than for agricultural commodities. Africa's share of the growing world market for iron ore is expected to increase, as has been shown by a study by the ECA which, on the whole, seems to take rather a pessimistic view of Africa's prospective share.[4] Copper is likely to remain a relatively scarce commodity for a long time to come and indeed Africa should be able to obtain a larger share of the growing world market. This is true not only of the existing producers, Zambia and the Democratic Republic of the Congo; more intensive prospection should make it possible for new producers to enter the market, e.g. Nigeria, the Republic of the Congo, the Central African Republic, and Mauritania.

Other commodities with good growth prospects in which Africa can hope to obtain a large share of the market through more intensive prospection and development are aluminium and tin, to say nothing of a number of semi-precious metals. One of the fundamental problems remains insufficient knowledge of Africa's mineral resources.

Little need be said of petroleum. All African countries with the slightest possibilities are naturally and rightly engaged in intensive prospection. The radical changes recently in the economic outlook of such countries as Algeria, Libya, Nigeria, and Gabon are well known.

The possibilities of markedly increasing the degree of processing of primary products before export are, from a technical and economic point of view, rather obvious: cocoa-butter and chocolate instead of cocoa; fish meal and fish flour; tinned meat; furniture instead of timber; margarine and soap instead of vegetable oils in their raw state; simple copper manufactures, and so forth. This problem occupied much of the attention of the 1964 UNCTAD. The tariff structures of the developed countries discriminate against first-stage processing of primary products and it is disturbing that so little progress has subsequently been made.

Three broad conclusions follow. The first is that wherever the long-run world market prospects for a commodity, whether agricultural or mineral, are good, it is to Africa's interest to intensify development for export as a means of earning foreign exchange; however, there is a corollary which is sometimes lost sight of—that it is not to Africa's interest to devote resources to the development of production for export of commodities where the world markets

are stagnant, or at best growing slowly.[5] Secondly, in the approach
to commodity arrangements Africa's interests are not necessarily
the same as those of other developing regions. Wherever she has a
comparative advantage it is sensible to press for arrangements
which are not unduly restrictive, so as to obtain the maximum
share of whatever market is likely to be available.[6] The third
conclusion is that however encouraging perspectives may be in
certain areas, the basic equation set out at the beginning of this
chapter concerning the relative rates of growth of markets for
commodities and manufactures remains valid, and thus the need
for a rapid structural change in African economies. This, therefore,
is the major thesis of the present study.

If, as will be argued, industrialization is the key to development,
it is essential first to dispose of a false antithesis between agriculture
and industry. The protagonists of industry rather than agriculture
have, on the face of it, much to be said on their side. After all, it is
a simple and well-established fact that whereas under-developed
countries employ 80 per cent or more of their population in agriculture, with a very small fraction in industry, developed countries employ in agriculture normally less than 20 per cent, down
to as low as 5 per cent. In its starkest terms economic development
is nothing more than the reversal of these proportions. Furthermore, under-developed countries are all too well aware of the
counsel they have so frequently received from politicians and
economists from industrialized countries, arguing that they should
not worry too much about industry but concentrate first on improving their agriculture.

The limitations on the prospects of a developing agricultural
production for export have already been shown. Yet the scope for
import substitution of food and agricultural raw materials in
Africa is almost as great as in industry. The message is much the
same as will be brought out later for industry, the need to increase
agricultural production for Africa's own markets, whether national
or multi-national.

The growth of industry requires increasing markets in the agricultural sector for capital goods such as agricultural implements
and machinery and for intermediate goods such as fertilizers and
pesticides, as well as for consumer goods. Agricultural production
has to increase not only to meet the growing needs of the agricultural sector itself but also increased demand in the industrial sec-

tor for food and raw materials as incomes rise and industrial production expands. Without this, as has been seen all too frequently in developing economies, the demand for imports increases rapidly and balance of payment problems intervene. It should also be remembered that for a considerable time to come industrialization is a means of increasing incomes and productivity but makes a relatively insignificant contribution to employment, since industry necessarily requires a relatively high capital intensity. Much of the increase in employment has to come from the modernization of the rural sector, including, as will be shown later, the physical infrastructure.

The interdependence of agriculture and industry can be summarized under six broad headings: agriculture as a supplier of food and raw materials; as an earner of foreign exchange; as a supplier of both capital and labour for industry; as a market for industrial products; as one of the main bases for industrialization in the form of agro-allied industries; and perhaps most important of all, the fact that it is the growing demand from the non-agricultural sectors which is the main stimulant of agricultural development itself.[7] The complementary nature of the relationship between agricultural and industrial development is now much better understood, but part of the continuing preoccupations of the pastoralists derives from what would seem to be an exaggeratedly pessimistic view of the recent agricultural performance in Africa.[8] Table 1 gives some recent estimates of annual growth rates of total agricultural production.

If it is true that there is little evidence of the transformation of traditional agricultural practices and organization, of the provisioning of urban and other developing centres, the qualitative improvement of diets, the further processing of crops especially for export, and the substitution of imported foods, it also remains true that there are no grounds for exaggerated pessimism or for believing that the tasks of agricultural development are such as to make impossible a complementary approach to both agriculture and industry.[9]

The next step, therefore, is to attempt to place industry within an appropriate strategy of economic development. A comprehensive reformulation of the theory of economic development in African terms has still to come. Nevertheless, the literature since the Second World War has provided many valuable clues. For

Table 1

ANNUAL GROWTH RATES OF TOTAL AGRICULTURAL
PRODUCTION
(percentages per year)

| Country | 1957–65 | Country | 1961–5 |
|---|---|---|---|
| Ivory Coast | 8·1 | Ivory Coast | 9·7 |
| Ghana | 7·0 | Tunisia | 9·7 |
| Ex-Federation | 5·5 | Morocco | 7·6 |
| Angola | 4·9 | Burundi | 6·6 |
| Kenya | 4·2 | Liberia ⎫ | |
| | | Ghana ⎬ | 4·8 |
| Sudan | 3·5 | UAR ⎫ | |
| Togo | 3·4 | Togo ⎬ | 4·3 |
| South Africa ⎫ | | | |
| Senegal ⎬ | 3·2 | Ex-Federation ⎫ | |
| Tanzania ⎫ | | Senegal ⎬ | 3·9 |
| Upper Volta ⎬ | 3·1 | Tanzania | 3·5 |
| Uganda ⎫ | | Madagascar | 3·1 |
| Mali ⎬ | 2·9 | Angola ⎫ | |
| UAR | | Uganda ⎬ | 2·6 |
| Nigeria ⎫ | | Cameroon ⎫ | |
| Cameroon ⎬ | 2·8 | Upper Volta ⎬ | 2·5 |
| Sierra Leone ⎭ | | Libya ⎭ | |
| Madagascar | 2·7 | Niger | 2·3 |
| Morocco ⎫ | | Nigeria | 2·2 |
| Niger ⎬ | 2·5 | | |
| | | Ethiopia | 1·5 |
| Ethiopia ⎫ | | Sierra Leone | 1·4 |
| Libya ⎬ | 1·9 | Algeria | 1·2 |
| Guinea | 1·7 | South Africa | 1·1 |
| Dahomey | 1·4 | Dahomey | 0·9 |
| Liberia | 0·8 | Sudan ⎫ | |
| Algeria | 0·5 | Mali ⎬ | 0·3 |
| Tunisia | 0·3 | Kenya | 0·0 |
| Rwanda | − 2·5 | Guinea | − 0·2 |
| Burundi | − 2·7 | Congo (Kinshasa) | − 2·6 |
| Congo (Kinshasa) | − 3·6 | Rwanda | − 5·6 |

*Source*: Calculated by Jack Dalton from 'Indices of Agricultural Production in 29 African Countries', USDA Economic Research Service,
December 1965, Washington, D.C.

present purposes it may be legitimate to summarize rather dog-matically the main elements of an approach.[10]

There has been increasing recognition that international spe-cialization in a free trading (non-discriminatory) world economy would not give rise automatically to equilibrium; on the con-trary, the gap between the rich and the poor nations tends to widen owing to the greater force in the developed world of what Myrdal has called 'backwash' effects compared with 'spread' effects, and the operation of his principle of 'cumulative causa-tion'.[11] Much of traditional theory assumes that resources in the form of capital, labour, technology, and skill are given, and for a long time economists were primarily concerned with price rela-tionships within a static equilibrium framework. Yet resources not only grow but grow unequally. Prebisch and the ECLA school have explained in detail the way in which under-developed countries depend for their export earnings on a limited range of primary products, and draw the appropriate policy conclusions: structural change, import substitution, industrialization under protection, and the export of manufactures.

The limits of import substitution in what has been called its 'easy' stage tend to be reached relatively quickly, as is the case in Latin America and India. On the other hand, Africa, with its high foreign trade independence, has still a long way to go. The follow-ing table shows imports into Africa over the last decade or more by main groupings. South Africa is excluded and the figures are expressed in millions of US dollars.

| | Total imports | Food, beverages, tobacco | | Other consumer goods | | Intermediate goods | | Capital goods | |
|---|---|---|---|---|---|---|---|---|---|
| | Value | Value | % | Value | % | Value | % | Value | % |
| 1954 | 4782 | 823 | 17·2 | 1520 | 31·8 | 1492 | 31·2 | 947 | 19·8 |
| 1958 | 6035 | 1074 | 17·8 | 1704 | 28·3 | 1975 | 32·7 | 1282 | 21·2 |
| 1960 | 6077 | 1133 | 18·6 | 1442 | 23·7 | 1699 | 28·0 | 1803 | 29·7 |
| 1963 | 6547 | 1328 | 20·3 | 1410 | 21·5 | 1867 | 28·5 | 1942 | 29·7 |
| 1964 | 7170 | 1431 | 20·0 | 1489 | 20·8 | 2050 | 28·6 | 2200 | 30·6 |

*Note:* The figures are drawn from official trade statistics and it should be noted that breakdowns for 1954 and 1958 are not strictly comparable with later years.

The figures show clearly the growing imports of food, beverages, and tobacco, the beginnings of an import substitution effect in other consumer goods, and steadily mounting imports of intermediate and capital goods. It should be noted that domestic passenger vehicles are included in capital goods.

At the same time, import substitution, at least of consumer goods, as a guide to policy, has its limits even in Africa. It does not explain industrial expansion but is merely one of its facets. As an approach it lays too much emphasis on present demand, rather than demand as it will or can be in the future as a result of development and structural change.

The post-war experience of Latin America has shown clearly that development geared on the one hand to exports of primary commodities and on the other to import substitution soon exhausts itself. The stage of easy import substitution for most Latin American countries is past. Imports are now approximately equal to 12 per cent of Latin America's overall income, compared with 28 per cent before the world depression—a measure of the progress made. Further substitution is becoming increasingly complex and costly, yet the problem of lack of foreign exchange continues to arise. 'The effect of import substitution as a means of correcting this disequilibrium does not last very long, for further increases in import demand, unaccompanied by a corresponding rise in exports, will once again lead to an external bottleneck.'[12] It has been pointed out, with the experience of Argentina especially in mind, that import substitution is a splendid device for substituting imports by imports.

It is true that on the face of it the contribution of import substitution in some Latin American countries has been impressive[13] and more will be said of the experience of selected Latin American countries in Chapter III. Thus, Baer and Kerstenetzky, analysing the changing structure of Brazilian industry between 1950 and 1960, show 'that the traditional industries of textiles, food products and clothing have suffered declines in relative position, while the most pronounced growth took place in such key import substituting industries as transport equipment, machinery, electric machinery and appliances and chemicals'.[14] They go on to point out that those industries which show the most import substitution are also those with the highest repercussions in the economy in terms of backward and forward linkages. This is surely stretching the term import substitution beyond the point where it has any precise meaning. What Brazil has been doing is to take significant steps towards changing the structure of her economy. In its literal sense, import substitution cannot do this. The past pattern of demand for consumer goods is a limited guide to the future, partly because there is or should be less emphasis on consumer goods and partly because some of the past imports are due to the existence of a well-to-do class and could now be reduced. By definition, the past can have little relevance to the future so far as intermediate and capital goods are concerned. Finally, the domestic manufacture of previously imported consumer goods, often at high cost behind substantial tariff walls, is likely to mean (unless it can be assumed that the whole of the investment is from abroad and that the investor in question is not prepared to invest in anything else) a diversion of scarce capital resources from the establishment of industries making intermediate and capital goods capable of changing the structure of the economy.[15]

When the limits of import substitution are reached, it becomes clear that export markets for manufactures have to be found, and this was a major theme of the Geneva World Trade Conference in 1964: the demand by the developing countries to force open the doors of the markets of the advanced countries. For African countries, at least for many years to come, there is an alternative approach: export of manufactures to each other. This is the underlying argument for the grouping of the markets of African nations and co-ordinated industrial development, the main thesis of Perroux[16] and the approach underlying much of the work of the ECA.

The reasons are not far to seek. On the one hand, whatever may be the prospects of Latin America or India, Africa can hardly hope to make much impact on the world market for manufactures for some time to come.

On the other, most African markets are small, partly as a result of the small population of many countries and also of the low income per head. Many industries cannot hope to be economic without a sizeable market, owing to the influence of economies of scale. The advantages of international specialization are clear. External economies plus linkage effects cannot be fully realized within the boundaries of single countries.

Perroux and his followers have also been primarily responsible for elaborating the growing point thesis,[17] the need to concentrate resources in a limited number of areas with a view to promoting self-sustaining growth and selecting the kind of industries which have genuine backward and forward linkage effects. Such possibilities are apparent in Africa within the framework of co-ordinated development among groups of countries. This in turn requires what the ECA has called sub-regional co-operation and an approach to free trade areas or common markets.

Yet there is a contradiction in this approach. Concentration of resources promotes faster growth, but there is also a tendency for the gap between the more and the less favoured countries or areas to grow. This is particularly apparent between the coastal and inland areas in West and Central Africa.[18] A solution to this dilemma has to be found. Even within a single developed country, marked regional differences arise which have persisted until there has been a large element of central government planning. Thus in France and the United Kingdom, serious attempts to tackle the problem date from after the Second World War. Throughout its history the USSR has endeavoured to correct the marked differences within its territory which stem from Tsarist times. Yet, despite all the efforts of the planners, the most industrialized parts of the country remain Moscow, Leningrad, and the Ukraine, even though the balance will continue to change.[19]

The primary role of industry in development is fully demonstrated from the lessons of history and, as has already been shown, is evident from the simple relationships of employment in agriculture and industry in developed and under-developed countries. Maizels, in his definitive statistical study, summarizes the evidence exhaustively.[20] He shows first of all that industrialization has been the key to economic progress in most countries and that the main reason is that industrialization tends to raise physical output per head. There are several reasons: the share of manufacturing in national output increases and the average product per worker is higher in manufacturing than in agriculture in low income economies; as industrialization proceeds, productivity in the manufacturing sector itself tends to increase relatively rapidly through economies of scale, increases in capital assets, and the development of new skills and attitudes to work; finally, productivity in the rest of the economy tends to rise as a result of industrialization, directly in the agricultural sector, as already shown, and indirectly through improved infrastructure, human and physical. Industrialization also changes the pattern of manufacturing output in response to changes in the structure of demand. There is a relatively rapid increase in the demand for capital goods, chemicals, and durable consumer goods, and a relatively slow expansion in the demand for food and textiles. As Maizels points out:

> The industrial development of the economically advanced countries provides empirical evidence of the existence of a common broad pattern of growth. . . . The results show a fairly sharp fall in the relative importance of food processing and textiles in the earlier stages of growth, with a continued, though reduced, rate of decline thereafter. Metals and engineering products show the reverse movement, with a declining rate of growth (relative to the total) as the later stages of development are reached. Chemical production shows an uninterrupted rise, while the miscellaneous group of manufactures first rises and then tends to fall slowly in relative importance.[21]

He goes on to point out that this well-established picture implies no precise rules about the stages of development of at present under-developed countries, and that the availability of aid and technical know-how, as well as other special features, makes possible changes in the pattern and thus acceleration of industrial growth and economic development.[22] Nevertheless, the broad lessons of the past concerning the place of industry in development and the general patterns of industrial growth are perfectly clear.

The essential point is that industry is the sole means of raising the productivity of an economy. This in turn determines the pattern of industrialization. The process depends partly on the linkage effects already referred to and therefore on a range of basic industries; partly on the transmission and creation of new technologies; and partly on the development of skill at all levels.

Despite the lessons of history, the path to industrialization has been the subject of controversy and some confusion, partly of a terminological character and partly owing to differing concepts. Frequently, distinctions made between large- and small-scale industry tend to be confusing, although it is clear that small-scale industry has a part to play, particularly in Africa—a subject which will be considered later. The distinction between heavy and light industry is sometimes obscure and the same applies to much of the discussion about the choice of technology.[23] For a considerable range of industry there is no real choice and this is particularly true of the kind of industry required to generate higher productivity throughout the economy, where capital intensity is normally of necessity high, frequently associated with economies in skilled labour.

There is a choice of technology and, therefore, in an under-developed country, it is obviously reasonable to apply labour-intensive methods in, for example, irrigation, road-building, housing, and construction in general. Technologically flexible industries include weaving, clothing, woodworking, leather, rubber products, some foodstuffs, bricks, tiles, some chemicals, and most of the simpler metal products. Comparatively low capital intensity is also required in such assembly industries as radios, TV, and bicycles. In such industries there is a case for seeing how far labour-intensive techniques are economic. They are not necessarily so. It is also possible to apply labour-intensive methods in ancillary operations, such as materials handling and packaging, in technologically inflexible industries.

The real issue remains the need, if serious development is contemplated, to launch a programme for the production of capital and intermediate goods, what de Bernis (following, of course, Marx) has called the production of machines which produce machines, with a view to changing the structure of the economy. As he also points out, much of the case for production of iron and steel and chemicals in Africa lies in the need to produce the inputs for agriculture: tools, implements, agricultural machinery, ferti-lizers, and insecticides. [24]

Although his thinking is close to that of de Bernis in many respects, Lacroix argues that the former's strategy, while probably appropriate to North Africa, is not realistic in the Congo and, by implication, in other tropical countries, especially in West and Central Africa. [25]

The controversy is a subtle one and a final answer can hardly be arrived at without more research in other African countries. De Bernis argues that what in effect amounts to priority for consumer goods in the first stage of industrialization is likely to mean a diversion of scarce investment resources away from intermediate and capital goods which alone can transform the structure of the economy and, above all, the agricultural sector. Lacroix argues that de Bernis puts too much emphasis on producing the inputs for agriculture and not enough on the demand side. If a higher proportion of agricultural output is to find its way on to the market, this means not only modern inputs but a basic social transformation,[26] and also the availability of goods for exchange arising from the industrial sector, in other words, consumer goods.

The conclusions to be drawn from the discussion are of limited practical significance so far as the Congo is concerned, since the first stage of import substitution (of consumer goods) has been largely realized and de Bernis and Lacroix are in complete agreement as to the prescriptions for the next stage. But the controversy is important in relation to the degree of priority for import substitution of consumer goods in other tropical African countries. There would seem to be a good deal to be said for de Bernis' view that virtually exclusive concentration on import substitution of consumer goods, many of which show little value added, must necessarily be at the expense of starting to lay down intermediate and capital goods (in small countries within the framework of the grouping of neighbours). There is bound to be *some* production of consumer goods, particularly those based on agricultural raw materials, just as there are bound to be *some* imports of consumer goods. It is a question of the appropriate proportion and in this context Lacroix is less than fair to de Bernis in suggesting that he is falling into the Nurkse error, i.e. the sidestepping of the fundamental economic problem of scarcity. The way out may lie partly in the suggestion that Lacroix himself puts forward that the Congo's neighbours in the UDEAC may be able to shorten the stage of substituting imports of consumer goods and begin immediately to think in terms of intermediate and capital goods (necessarily on a group basis) by importing consumer goods already being produced in the Congo.

The major issue remains the structural transformation of Africa. Hence, in classifying industries from the point of view of development, the real distinction is between capital, intermediate, and consumer goods. The perspectives, through rapid industrialization, were first sketched out by the ECA.[27] It was argued that Africa could reach broadly the present levels of economic development of Western Europe by the end of the present century if it were to double its agricultural output and multiply by 25 times its industrial output per capita. The implications of such a structural change would be that the share of agriculture in GDP would fall from 35 to 20 per cent by the end of the century and that of industry would rise from 20 to 40 per cent. Total industrial output would have to rise at about 8 per cent per annum from 1960 to 1980 and thereafter at 9 per cent, with a rate of growth of mining somewhat lower and of manufacturing somewhat higher. Within the manufacturing group light industry would have to expand significantly more slowly than heavy industry, in line with historical experience, as already shown. The detailed implications of this scheme are shown in Chapter IV.

There are twenty-three countries in Africa each with a population of 4 million or less; twelve with less than 2 million, and seven with less than 1 million. Since in addition incomes per head are very low, it soon becomes evident that the industrial development indicated above is impossible in the African context without the grouping of countries. The basic reasons are, first, economies of scale. The minimum scale of output for much basic industry is relatively high. Thus a modern integrated iron and steel works, even if it concentrates on light steel products, requires a minimum output of about half a million ingot tons. Optimum scales of output are much higher, e.g. a wide strip mill, 5 million ingot tons; a multi-product integrated mill, 3·5 million ingot tons; and a non-integrated mill, 1 million ingot tons. Ammonia, required for the production of nitrogen fertilizer, can be produced reasonably economically at a minimum of 50,000 tons, although there are great savings if the level can be substantially raised. The figures are lower for basic acids and alkalis, but still large in relation to African markets, i.e. from 5,000 to 10,000 tons for sulphuric, nitric, and hydrochloric acid and caustic soda. Basic chemicals and fertilizers, normally the first objectives of a chemical industry in a developing country, require combinations or complexes. Surpluses or by-products arise when a given main product is produced which require proper outlets for the whole plant to be economic, e.g. chlorine when caustic soda is produced, which can, however, be turned into pesticides or plastic raw material (PVC). The generally accepted minimum scale of output for an integrated pulp and paper mill is about 40,000 tons; that for flat glass is of the order of 10,000 tons. Cement can be produced on a comparatively small scale owing to the protection offered by high transport costs, although there are marked economies as capacity rises. Textiles can be produced fairly cheaply on a moderately small scale, except viscose rayon, which requires a minimum output of 20,000 to 30,000 tons. On the other hand, the range of finished products turned out by the textile industry is large, so that a full range of them is inconceivable without a large market. There are clear gains from international specialization. There is a much wider range of minimum scales of output in the metal manufactures group and production is economic on a relatively small scale for a wide range of metal products and small electrical goods. Assembly of transport equipment is frequently undertaken on a small scale, but the prospects of moving progressively into the manufacture of components depend upon access to wide markets. Heavy electrical machinery, machine tools, and almost all kinds of specialized industrial equipment also require large markets.

What this means in terms of prospective African markets ten and fifteen years from now is discussed in some detail in Chapter IV. It will suffice here to give a few illustrations of market size, on the assumption that African countries continue to try to industrialize largely in isolation from each other, and in terms of their prospective demand in about 1970, the end of the period of most existing African development plans. Assuming, for this illustration, no exports outside Africa, only the UAR could support a viable iron and steel industry, a nitrogen fertilizer plant, a caustic soda/chlorine complex, a pulp and paper mill, and flat glass manufacture. No country could support more than relatively simple mechanical and electrical engineering products. About half could not progress beyond the simplest types of metal product, and several would not have a large enough market for a cement plant.

The role of economies of scale in promoting growth has received powerful support from Kaldor in the inaugural lecture attached to his chair of economics at Cambridge, where he described the economies of scale in industry as 'the main engine of growth'.[28] Furthermore, it is not simply a question of the optimum size of an industry but of achieving the optimum scale of output at each stage in the process of production in a given industry. For example, in the early fifties the wide strip mill in Western Europe operated inefficiently, because the capacity for producing crude steel and slabs, and at the finishing stages, was below and out of balance with that for producing hot rolled coils.[29] Subsequent selective investment led to great increases in output and reduced costs. In most African countries it is not so much a question at present of

c

optimum scales of output as of attaining the minimum economic size appropriate to each industry. Even to achieve this, as has been shown, the grouping of countries is required. But the principles are the same, including the balancing of the stages in the production process, which can be of even greater importance in a developing country.

Needless to say, there remains a large range of industry where small-scale production is perfectly feasible, partly because the economies-of-scale factor is unimportant—many small-scale industries are a means of transition—and partly because of the association between large- and small-scale industry and the sub-contracting factor. Even in the United States a significant part of industrial output continues to be contributed by small industries.[30] This problem will be considered later in discussing the instruments of industrial development. Yet it will be evident that reliance mainly on small industry is insufficient if the strategic industries essential for the structural transformation of an economy are to be envisaged.

The second reason for the grouping of economies follows from the first, economies of scale: namely, the advantages of division of labour and international specialization.

The third factor has already been discussed earlier in this chapter, the scope for taking advantage of external economies and linkages which arises from the grouping of economies. Industrialization is much more than establishing at random a collection of industries. Hirschman, drawing on statistics prepared by Chenery and Watanabe presenting interdependence data obtained from United States, Japanese, and Italian experience which show that the industries with the highest combined forward and backward linkages are iron and steel, non-ferrous metals, paper, petroleum and coal products, chemicals, and textiles, demonstrates why these are the strategic industries in a developing economy.[31]

The arguments for the grouping of African economies as an essential condition of industrial development are overwhelming. Yet, as recent experience has shown, there are immense difficulties in reaching agreement in practice. This problem will be examined in Chapter V, together with arrangements which have been made or are being considered. Suffice to say here that it is now generally accepted that an under-developed country has to protect its infant industries from foreign competition by restricting imports, since normally, despite low wages, real costs initially are high. It follows that within a system of grouped countries the protective tariff has to be applied on a regional or sub-regional basis, with free trade within the group at least for the products of the industries serving the whole market.[32] Protection of the infant industries is required to offset the differences between private and social costs, since the marginal private costs of production are higher, relative to the marginal social costs, than in a developed country. This argument goes back to List, though its general acceptance is comparatively recent.

It has recently been strongly reinforced owing to the recognition of widespread unemployment or under-employment in under-developed countries. If there is no alternative employment available, the opportunity cost of drawing such labour into industry is zero. Hence the case for shadow or accounting prices—which are, of course, less than current market prices—in determining the viability of an industrial project.[33]

The argument so far has been based on the necessity for and perspectives of industrialization. Yet to demonstrate this is not nearly enough and is certainly no guarantee that industrialization will take place. It is obvious, of course, that financial resources are required. But even if capital is forthcoming, this also is not sufficient. A real industrial development strategy requires not only the right perspectives geared to the structural transformation of the economy but also fulfilment of the prerequisites of industrial development and the calling forth of the agents of development: in other words, knowledge and its application, and people. These problems are examined in the seventh and eighth chapters of this book.

## NOTES AND REFERENCES TO CHAPTER I

[1] See *Towards a New Trade Policy for Development: Report by the Secretary General of the United Nations Conference on Trade and Development*, United Nations, New York, 1964.

[2] The latest, on the whole rather gloomy assessment, without however making specific forecasts, can be found in the UNCTAD Commodity Survey 1966 (for a summary see TD/B/c.1/23/Add. 3, December 1966). Difficulties now arising, particularly in the markets for sugar, cocoa, coffee, iron ore, tin, lead, zinc, copper, rubber, and hard fibres, are examined.

[3] FAO Commodity Review, 1962; Special Supplement entitled *Agricultural Commodities—Projections for 1970*.

[4] To be published.

[5] J. W. F. Rowe severely criticizes the use of commodity control schemes to bolster up prices artificially high and thus encourage the waste of resources, pointing out the dangers of using these schemes as a disguised form of giving aid indirectly rather than giving aid directly. He makes the important distinction between commodity control schemes as such, as a means of regulating markets, but which should not be employed to keep prices artificially high; and the type of compensatory scheme discussed at the Geneva conference, designed to offset short-term falls in earnings, to which contributions may be made from producers and consumers alike, and which he considers a perfectly legitimate device (J. W. F. Rowe, *Primary Commodities in International Trade*, Cambridge, 1965, pp. 215 ff.).

[6] Rowe gives a good example in criticizing the 1962 Coffee Agreement which was a deliberate device to maintain Brazil's prices artificially high (promoted by the United States as what he considers to have been a deliberate weapon in the cold war). One consequence was the maintaining of obsolescent high-cost capacity and the prevention of expansion of new low-cost industries 'such as the African industry in Kenya' (ibid., p. 181).

[7] This problem is discussed lucidly in the *State of Food and Agriculture*, FAO, Rome, 1966, Chap. III, although there is perhaps insufficient emphasis on the parallel to develop capital goods within the framework of the grouping of African markets.

[8] Derived from the Economic Research Service of the US Department of Agriculture.

[9] It is only fair to add that there are those who are beginning to argue that within the whole perspective of world development the comparative advantage of developing countries in manufactures may become greater than in agriculture. Lewis, for example, has said: 'Some of us believe even that the time is not far off when the under-developed countries will be net importers of primary products, and net exporters of manufactures' ('A Review of Economic Development', Richard T. Ely Lecture, *American Economic Review*, Vol. IV, No. 2, May 1965). A correspondent in *The Economist* (28 May–3 June 1966) has presented this type of thesis even more forcefully, basing himself on the increasingly capital intensive nature of agriculture in the advanced countries, the physical and natural advantages of the temperate zones, and the sheer difficulty of raising agricultural productivity particularly in the under-developed tropical zones. These difficulties are also examined by Dumont in the African context (*Développement agricole africain*, Presses Universitaires de France, Paris, 1965) but his conclusions are more positive in terms of prospects of African agricultural development. A detailed examination of these problems is outside the scope of the present study.

[10] Detailed references are not given here. An attempt has been made elsewhere to review recent contributions (see A. F. Ewing, 'Some Recent Contributions to the Literature on Economic Development', *Journal of Modern African Studies*, Vol. 4, No. 3 (which includes some fifty-odd references).

[11] G. Myrdal, *An International Economy*, London, 1956; *Economic Theory and Under-Developed Regions*, London, 1957.

[12] R. Prebisch, *Towards A Dynamic Development Policy for Latin America*, United Nations (Sales No. 64. II. 9.4), New York, 1963.

[13] For a detailed account, see *The Economic Development of Latin America in the Post-War Period*, United Nations (Sales No. 64.II.9. 6), New York, 1964.

[14] W. Baer and I. Kerstenetzky, 'Import Substitution and Industrialization in Brazil', *American Economic Review*, Vol. LIV, No. 3, March 1964, p. 416. See also Baer, *Industrialization and Economic Development in Brazil*, Homewood, Illinois, 1965, Chap. 6.

[15] Chudson points out that the textile industries in Africa seem to require protection well above average, particularly against Indian exports, and are likely to remain non-competitive for a long time to come (see W. A. Chudson, 'Comparative Costs and Economic Development: The African Case', *American Economic Review*, ibid., p. 407. Textiles are a good example of an easy import substitution industry where economies of scale are not too important. It by no means follows that most African countries should lay down textiles, often at the expense of potentially more productive industries from the point of view of the economy as a whole.

[16] F. Perroux, *L'Économie des jeunes nations*, Paris, 1962.

[17] F. Perroux, 'Note sur la notion de "Pôles de croissance"', *Économie appliquée*, Paris, Vol. VIII, No. 1–2.

[18] This is also a serious problem in Brazil where despite extensive special programmes for the north-east, the gap between this and the central-south continues to widen (see Baer, *Industrialization and Economic Development in Brazil*, op. cit.).

[19] See *Economic Survey of Europe in 1959*, ECE, Geneva, 1960.

[20] A. Maizels, *Industrial Growth and World Trade*, Cambridge, 1963.

[21] Ibid. p. 9.

[22] An interesting exception is South Africa (see *Economic Survey of Africa*, ECA, UN Sales No. II. K.3, New York, 1966). The share of investment goods and metals is nearly twice as large in manufacturing output as the normal for a country of this size and income. In fact, it corresponds to an income three times as large. Textiles, and still more food, drink, and tobacco, are abnormally low, owing to the extremely unequal distribution of income. Thus the South African economy is for its level of development at one and the same time structurally advanced and distorted. This, as the ECA Survey points out, will lead to serious difficulties and further tensions as South Africa becomes more and more isolated from the rest of Africa.

[23] Dobb refers to the fact that much literature assumes that the choice of technique should depend on the existing factor endowment in a country at any particular stage of development and also states that it should be unnecessary to point out that the choice of technology for a given investment and the distribution of investment are quite distinct issues (see M. H. Dobb, *Economic Growth and Planning*, New York, 1960, pp. 33 and 65). He also points out, however, that the same grounds which justify a high rate of investment also justify a high degree of capital intensity in the choice of the form of investment (see 'A Note on the so-called Degree of Capital Intensity of Investment in Under-developed Countries', *Économie appliquée*, Paris, 1954).

[24] G. de Bernis, '*Industrie lourde et industrie légère*', in *Industrialisation au Maghreb*, Paris, 1963.

[25] See J. L. Lacroix, *Industrialisation au Congo: la transformation des structures*

*économiques*, Éditions Mouton, Paris, 1967. See also a review of this work by the present writer, which has been drawn upon here, in the *Journal of Modern African Studies*, Vol. 4, No. 2. See also a more extended review in *Cahiers économiques et sociaux*, Vol. IV, No. 4.

[26] See in this context E. Younes and G. Berrebi: '*Les places respectives de la réforme agraire et de l'industrialisation dans la stratégie de développement économique*', in *Agriculture, Land Reforms, and Economic Development*, Polish Scientific Publishers, Warsaw, 1964. The authors have in mind particularly Tunisian experience and criticize de Bernis partly on the same grounds as Lacroix. However, the particular land reform problem the authors have in mind is not of much relevance in tropical Africa.

[27] *Industrial Growth in Africa*, United Nations (Sales No. 62. II. K.3), New York, 1963, p. 14. The methodology for the calculations in this study relating to industrial growth perspectives in Africa was derived from S. J. Patel's path-breaking article,' Economic Distance between Nations: The Origin, Measurement and Outlook', first contributed to the *Economic Journal* and reprinted in *Essays in Economic Transition*, Bombay, 1965. See also the papers prepared by de Bernis and his colleagues for a series of conferences on 'The Harmonization of Industrial Development in West Africa' convened by the President of Niger between 1962 and 1964; *The Growth of World Industry 1953–65*, United Nations (Sales No. 63. XVII. 10); and *A Study of Industrial Growth*, United Nations (Sales No. 63. II. B.2), New York.

[28] See *The Economist*, 5 November 1966, p. 548.

[29] See *The European Steel Industry and the Wide Strip Mill*, New York, 1952.

[30] For an exhaustive discussion of the role of small-scale industries, see E. Staley and R. Morse, *Modern Small Industry for Developing Countries*, Stanford Research Institute, New York, 1965.

[31] A. O. Hirschman, *The Strategy of Economic Development*, Yale, 1958.

[32] Cf. J. Ilett, 'Designated Product Common Markets', *The East African Economics Review*, December, 1962.

[33] See also Chapter VII.

# CHAPTER II

# THE PRESENT PATTERN OF INDUSTRY IN AFRICA

In this chapter the present pattern of industry in Africa is described. This is followed by a comparative analysis of performance and policies in selected countries. An assessment of the present pattern is far from easy, owing to lack of sufficient and comparable industrial statistics. An attempt can be made on the basis of the quantitative data available and judgement based on the methodological approach set out in the first chapter.

As a starting-point it may be useful to give some broad economic indicators, well enough known but important to recall, drawn from various United Nations sources. Africa in 1960 accounted for about 8 per cent of the world's population (273 million out of 3,000 million). Its average income per head (US dollars about 110–120) is about one-twelfth of that of the average of the industrialized countries. Although it possesses 28 per cent of the estimated world electric power potential it has only one per cent of installed capacity. Over half of its secondary sector is accounted for by mining for export, compared with 8 per cent in the industrialized countries. Total African employment in mining and manufacturing taken together is only one and a half million. In most African countries manufacturing accounts for only a few per cent of GDP. At current prices, while output per head in agriculture (in terms of total population) is three times as much in the industrialized countries as in Africa, it is thirty times as much in industry.

It is possible, on the basis of some 140–150 industries, classified under ten industrial groupings, to produce an approximate picture of the present state of industrial development. The groupings are: food, textiles and allied industries, forest industries, non-metallic minerals, metals, chemicals and fertilizers, metal products, mechanical industries, electrical industries, and transport equipment. These groupings cover not only the whole range of industry already installed in at least one African country but all that is likely to be possible for the next two decades. The 140–150 industries covered are in a sense arbitrary. A more detailed breakdown is theoretically possible. All that can be said is that the same breakdown has been employed throughout. The picture is open to an obvious objection, that a given industry in one country may mean one small plant and, in another, a considerable number of plants. Nevertheless, this approach has the merit, at least, of showing the industrial structure, actual or potential, in each country. The detailed data used are not reproduced here, partly because it is not the intention in this study to include extensive descriptive material and partly because any chart of this kind might encourage the drawing of misleading conclusions.[1]

Bearing in mind these limitations, it may be noted that the number of industries installed in all 36 independent countries of Africa in mid-1966, together with Mauritius and Rhodesia, varies from 115 in the UAR to 3 in Mauritania. There are nine countries in the top quartile: Algeria, the Democratic Republic of the Congo, the Ivory Coast, Kenya, Morocco, Nigeria, Rhodesia, Tunisia, and the UAR. The variation is between 115 and 53. There are nine countries in the lowest quartile: Burundi, Gabon, Mali, Mauritania, Niger, Rwanda, Somalia, Togo, and Upper Volta, varying from 13 to 3.

Nearly all African countries, whatever their size or level of development, have installed or are in the process of installing the following industries: flour milling, beer and beverages, clothing, boots and shoes, sawn wood and joinery, including wooden furniture, plastic manufactures, soap, liquid air, paint, metal products for construction, household utensils, repair of motor vehicles, and, where appropriate, repair of railway equipment or small ships. These are typical import substitution industries, largely consumer goods and to a limited extent simple intermediate goods.

The range of food industries installed is considerably greater from the point of view of Africa as a whole, and the specific industries depend on the agricultural resources of the country in question, e.g. sugar, edible oils, processed meat, dairy products, tinned fruit and fruit juices, canned vegetables, and processed rice. The development of forest industries in certain countries is obviously also a function of forest resources and has led, therefore, to production in some of them of veneers and plywood, pulp and paper, and packaging. The same by and large is true of textiles and cement.

So far fertilizers are produced only in North Africa, and the

same is true of a limited range of basic chemicals. Otherwise
chemical products in Africa at present mean little more than insecticides, explosives, liquid air, paints, distilleries, perfume, sulphuric acid, and matches; and frequently only the final preparation of products is undertaken.

The base metal industries hardly exist outside North Africa,
other than limited re-rolling of steel and the production for export
of copper, cobalt, zinc, tin, lead, and aluminium.

As has been seen, almost all countries have made at least a start
in the field of metal products, although there are few producing
the more advanced elements such as heavy steel structures, tanks,
vats, boilers, and gas cylinders, cans and metal boxes, cables and
ropes, agricultural equipment, and tubes. Mechanical engineering
hardly exists outside the UAR, and the same is largely true of
electrical equipment other than for household uses. Transport
equipment, again apart from the UAR, means essentially assembly
or repair.

Finally, it should be noted that even among the range of consumer goods and intermediate goods to be found at least on some
scale in almost all countries, the value added domestically is for the
most part limited. Thus beer and beverages are frequently based
on imported materials and bottles. The same is true of paint.
Clothing industries are generally on a small scale, based on imported cloth. The boot and shoe industry is heavily weighted in
favour of plastics drawn from imported raw materials; in the case
of leather, tanning materials are imported. Almost all metal products are based on imported metal.

This impressionistic picture of the present degree of industrial
development in Africa, together with other available data, makes
it possible to set out a number of broad generalizations.

In the first place there is a limited degree of correlation between
the levels of GDP per head and the present state of African industrialization. The latest available figures of GDP per head, expressed
in US dollars, show five countries with over 200: Gabon, Ghana,
Libya, Rhodesia, and Zambia. Of these only Rhodesia is in the
upper quartile in terms of the range of industry installed. Gabon is
in the lower quartile, and the other three are well down in the
median bracket. Some of the relatively high figures are the result
of exploitation of mining or petroleum resources. Thus, Libya has
become a major oil producer, Gabon is a major mining and timber

producer, and Zambia a major mining producer. The same applies to a number of countries in the next GDP bracket, all with little industry, e.g. Guinea, Liberia, Mauritania, and Sierra Leone. The relatively high GDP figures for Ghana and Senegal stem largely from cocoa and groundnuts respectively.

A relative development of the industrial structure and the converse on the part of neighbours is partly accounted for by the position of certain countries in past or present customs unions, e.g. Kenya, Rhodesia, and Senegal.

Leaving aside mineral resources, which have been a factor in the prosperity of certain countries, owing to overseas export, a leading factor accounting for present patterns of industrialization has been the presence of specific agricultural resources, e.g. fish, meat, and tropical agricultural products.

Even though GDP per head is low, a sizeable market as a result of a large or relatively large population has been an important factor in accounting for a reasonably large range of industry. This is evidently the case in the UAR, although there are other factors, and also in Nigeria, the Democratic Republic of the Congo, and to some extent Ethiopia.

Two countries may be regarded as in some degree special cases, the UAR and the Democratic Republic of the Congo, both of which will be considered in more detail at a later stage. The former has the advantage of a large population, a fairly long period of independence, a relatively advanced educational system, the emergence of an entrepreneurial class, and deliberate measures on the part of the planning authorities to change the structure of the economy. In the case of the Democratic Republic of the Congo, in addition to a fair-sized market there is a special factor: the fact that this country has long had its own currency and equal treatment of importers, thus promoting local enterprise, although admittedly foreign-owned, under conditions of competition.

It is possible, on the basis of the foregoing considerations, to classify forty-one African countries from the point of view of industrial development into three main groups. In the first group are small countries where industrialization can hardly be said to have started. In this group are: Botswana, Burundi, the Central African Republic, Chad, the Republic of the Congo, Dahomey, Gabon, the Gambia, Guinea, Lesotho, Liberia, Libya, Madagascar, Malawi, Mali, Mauritania, Mauritius, Niger, Rwanda,

Sierra Leone, Somalia, the Sudan, Swaziland, Tanzania, Togo, Uganda, Upper Volta, and Zambia.

The second group of countries, all of which have a fair-sized population and three of which are quite large, have already installed a certain range of industry, although mainly consumer goods and a limited range of intermediate goods. Yet in all of them the industrialization process either shows signs of coming to a halt or such a stage can be foreseen in the relatively near future. In this group are: Algeria, the Cameroon, the Democratic Republic of the Congo, Ethiopia, Ghana, the Ivory Coast, Kenya, Morocco, Nigeria, Rhodesia, and Senegal.

In the third category are countries which have begun to change the structure of their economies and to lay down on a significant scale intermediate goods and some capital goods. There are only two countries at present in this group, Tunisia and the UAR.

### INDUSTRIAL DEVELOPMENT BY COUNTRIES

In the next stage of the analysis more detailed consideration will be given to the state of industrialization, its structure, and the immediate future plans of selected countries. Five countries will be examined in the first group: the Republic of the Congo, Guinea, Mali, Tanzania, and Uganda. They have been chosen largely because there is evidence of dynamic leadership and attempts to promote rapid industrialization. It follows that these are the most favourable examples of countries in the first group. In the second group, the Cameroon, the Democratic Republic of the Congo, Ethiopia, Kenya, Ghana, the Ivory Coast, Morocco, Nigeria, and Senegal will be examined, as will also the two countries in the third group, Tunisia and the UAR.

Although the intention in each case is to show briefly the state of industry in each country considered and the policies or plans of the governments, industry cannot be considered in isolation. Consequently, something must also be said about the social and political background, the state of physical and human infrastructure, agriculture, and the approach to development planning.[2]

The *Republic of the Congo* has a population of less than one million, but is fairly well endowed with natural resources, agricultural and mineral, and has a relatively well-developed infrastructure. Brazzaville was the capital of former French Equatorial Africa and has therefore the necessary attributes in administrative and financial facilities, together with educational institutions, intended to serve and still in some measure serving the four countries. It has a development plan which expires in 1968, drawn up on classical French lines and, so far as industry is concerned, largely a framework for foreign private enterprise. The present government may be regarded as left wing in orientation in its general political philosophy but has so far shown little sign of attempting to adopt a State-directed approach to industrialization.

The country has a considerable range of food industries, notably in the valley of the Niari, under the control of the French concern SIAN. Sugar is being produced on a large scale, with the intention of developing exports to other French-speaking African countries. There is marked potential for the production of fruit and vegetables and one of the objectives is large-scale production of canned fruit juice for export. The Republic of the Congo is also well endowed with forest resources and is a significant exporter of timber and timber products. There is a fair range of the simpler metal products and such chemical industries as liquid air, paint, and perfume. Intermediate and capital goods industries are barely represented.

Among the current industrial development projects either under way or envisaged, apart from the food and forest industries, are large-scale production of potash for export and an ambitious plan for the harnessing of the Sounda barrage with a view to producing aluminium and ferro-alloys for export. It is also hoped to mine and export on a large scale iron ore, of which there are rich deposits. A cement works is under construction. But this apart, there are no serious plans at present for the production of intermediate and capital goods. Clearly, for this to be possible, would require close co-operation with the neighbouring countries of Central Africa, a problem which will be discussed later. However, as will be seen, present industrial policy, apart from limited import substitution, is based essentially on a traditional approach: export overseas of raw materials.

*Guinea* has a population of about 3·5 million and is outside the French monetary zone. From independence it opted for radical social change in its approach to education, tribalism, the position of women, and the role of the State in economic development. It is an essentially agricultural country, exporting coffee, bananas, and palm kernels, but is still compelled to import a high proportion of food for domestic consumption. However, it is now taking steps to diversify agriculture and is expected within a few years to be able to feed itself. It is well endowed with mineral resources, being a major exporter of bauxite and alumina, and a significant exporter of iron ore, with rich deposits still untapped. It also has extensive hydro-electrical resources, which it plans to exploit on a large scale, in the first instance mainly in order to produce aluminium for export.

Manufacturing industry has been little developed and includes the usual range of first-stage industries—textiles, cigarettes, matches, a cannery, a sawmill, bricks, and furniture. It is planned to lay down a sugar refinery and a second cannery. The country has ambitions to produce iron and steel, but this is unlikely for some time to come and possible only within the framework of co-operation with its neighbours.

Ambitious targets were adopted in the first development plan, covering the period 1959–63, involving an increase in the index for agriculture of 150 and for industry of 800, and an overall growth rate of 15 per cent. The three-year plan was quite independent of the FRIA programme for the production of alumina. Stage 1, which was attained in 1963, was 480,000 tons; stage 2 envisages increased production of alumina to 720,000 tons, and stage 3, de-pending on the setting up of the Souapiti barrage, envisages 150,000 tons of aluminium. The FRIA project is a typical example of an enclave. It has been calculated that barely 12 per cent of the investment expenses in the construction period affected the internal Guinean economy. As to benefits at the operating stage, ex-ports of 6·8 milliard francs have been offset by imports for the project and financial transfers abroad amounting to 5·6 milliard frs, leaving 1·7 milliard frs (one milliard in taxes and the remain-der in local purchases).[3]

The industrial targets in the plan proper were seriously under-fulfilled, the index amounting to only 200. During the period, GNP rose by 9·2 per cent per annum, but if the FRIA project is excluded, the rate of growth was only 4 per cent.[4] The principal reasons for the relative failure in Guinea and the complete lack of progress so far towards changing the structure of the economy, as envisaged in the plan and despite a radical political approach in theory, seem to have been the inflation of administrative expendi-ture, as in many other African countries; the failure to tackle effectively *encadrement rural* in the agricultural sector; and the inability to prepare realistic industrial projects.

*Mali* has a population of over 4 million and its territory is one of the largest in West Africa. Like Guinea, Mali has also attempted to promote a forward-looking social policy and has put much emphasis on the role of the State in economic development. Like Guinea also, it has its own currency, although some links have been maintained with the franc zone and it may return to the CFA franc.

Traditionally, cattle raising has been a major element in the economy, with exports of cattle or meat to the Ivory Coast and Ghana markets, which are now threatened by the development of intensive cattle raising in these two countries. Other traditional exports are groundnuts, groundnut oil, and cotton.

Until independence, industry in Mali was virtually negligible, but a considerable effort has been made subsequently and some range of traditional import substitution industries has now been established, including a considerable number of food industries and some of the simpler metal products. The current industrial development effort is along the same lines, and industries under construction or being seriously studied include cotton seed oil, refined sugar, further development of meat, including dairy products, rice processing, saw-milling, textiles, hosiery, sack-making, plastics manufactures, cement, ceramics and refractory bricks, agricultural equipment, and the assembly of transistor radios. There is also a plan to establish an iron and steel works, but this depends on a firm agreement with neighbouring countries and the building of the barrage at Gouina, which cannot be expected before the seventies.

The effort made within a short space of time in Mali is noteworthy, but, again, it will be seen that for some years to come there will be only limited development of intermediate and capital goods and that such is evidently impossible without co-operation with neighbouring countries, a point much more fully appreciated by the Malian than by the Guinean authorities. Another positive feature is the emphasis that has been placed in recent years on mineral surveying as a basis for substantial industrialization at a later stage.

As in other countries, administrative expenses have increased at a rapid rate and there have been a number of extravagant infrastructural projects—official buildings, hotels, airports. Further-more, little progress has been made to transform methods of pro-duction in agriculture, owing to insufficient *encadrement rural*.[5]

*Tanzania* has a population of about 10 million and, as will be discussed more fully later, was the poor relation in the British East African Common Market. With a vast territory and relatively under-developed communications, together with harsher climatic conditions than its neighbours, it entered into independence with a very limited degree of industrialization. However, it enjoyed the advantage of a unifying political force in the Tanganyika African National Union, which had been preparing for independence for some years before this was achieved.

At independence, industries were confined to some of the tradi-tional food products, limited forest industries, textiles, clothing and boots and shoes, building materials, including cement, and some of the simpler metal products.

The development plan, covering the period 1964–69, is one of the best designed in Africa, in its conception and strategy, the ambition of its growth rates, and its general coherence. There is an explicit development strategy with the main emphasis on struc-tural change, covering *inter alia* the rapid expansion of modern industry, including increased output per capita, massive expansion of the educational system, emphasis on high and middle level man-power, higher investment in relation to the national product sup-ported by even greater increases in national savings, a radical in-crease in the role of the State, reduced relative dependence on exports of primary products, national control over economic policy decisions at all levels as distinct from leaving the execution of the plan largely to foreign investors, modernization of agriculture, re-duction in inequality of income distribution, and joint develop-ment with neighbouring countries.[6]

The plan is conceived as the first of a series. It is envisaged that the proportion of domestic output accounted for by agriculture will fall from 57·4 per cent in 1960–62 to 37·3 per cent in 1980 and that the proportion accounted for by industry will rise from 12·8 to 26·7 per cent. The rate of growth of agriculture is planned to be between 4 and 5 per cent and of industry between 10 and 12 per cent, with the rate of growth of GDP 6·7 per cent.

It is, of course, too soon to give any indication of how these ambitious targets are being realized in practice. Furthermore, the high growth rates in industry necessarily assume the steady laying down of intermediate and capital goods, which in turn requires genuine harmonization of industrial planning with neighbouring countries in East Africa. Nevertheless, it is clear that in intention at least the Government is determined to carry through a genuine strategy of industrial development.

A new plan has recently been published for *Uganda* covering the period 1966–81. The emphasis is on a growing share of industry and construction, including a shift to export processing and food manufactures. At the same time, agriculture is not neglected, through modern inputs and credit facilities. The GDP growth rate is planned to rise to 6·3 per cent during the period 1966–71 and 7·1 per cent in the following decade. A higher rate of investment is planned. It is hoped to hold the per capita increase in incomes down to 2·5 per cent per annum, implying a severe policy of income restraint.[7] Five major structural changes are envisaged. First, the increase in the share of investment, which has one implication already referred to, the holding down of increases in consumption, and another, a marked reliance on public investment. Furthermore, construction is to become a key sector, partly because of its capacity for employment creation. It is estimated that for every £1,000,000 worth of construction, 3,000 workers are employed, twice as many as in other non-agricultural sectors. Secondly, there is to be a shift within the agricultural sector towards domestic markets, despite the intention to expand absolutely the volume of agricultural exports. Thirdly, there is marked emphasis on import substitution not only of consumer but also of intermediate goods, making it possible for capital goods to rise from less than one-sixth to over one-third of total imports. Fourthly, average tax rates are to be increased by 30 per cent over the next five years. Fifthly, a dramatic expansion of secondary and higher education is planned, including a rate of increase of entrance to university from 1965 to 1978 of 27 per cent a year.[8] The new plan, which represents a marked break with previous thinking, puts Uganda, so far as planning conception is concerned, among the advanced countries of Africa.

In the next group of countries the range of industries already established is of course greater. *Kenya* has a number of food industries, forest industries, a considerable degree of development of textiles, clothing, boots and shoes, sack-making, and string and rope. Most non-metallic minerals are represented, the simpler chemicals and metal products, together with agricultural implements, diesel engines, pumps, and valves. Kenya, as will be seen later, has benefited from a privileged position in the East African Common Market. Nevertheless, a start only has been made with intermediate goods and there is a virtual absence of capital goods.

Independence in Kenya was achieved relatively late and with some difficulty, owing partly to European settlement and partly to tribal problems. Agriculture has been relatively well developed owing largely to the modern techniques introduced by the white farmers. It is argued that the transition to Africanization of agriculture has led, in the short run at least, to a considerable fall in agricultural productivity. Production has not fallen throughout the agricultural sector, e.g. coffee and tea, where there has been increased production by Africans and where, under the aegis of the Kenya Tea Development Authority, Africans, as individuals or on a co-operative basis, have made considerable progress. Furthermore, there are other factors which have led to a fall in agricultural productivity, e.g. the wait-and-see attitude of the European farmers who would like to stay in Kenya and early panic on the part of some of them who sold their farms at a time when there were no other arrangements ready for management.

The approach to national planning is in marked contrast to Tanzania's. The main strategy is based on a rapid increase in the African share of the national product, a political necessity; emphasis on agriculture, partly because this is the simplest approach to Africanization, and secondary emphasis on manufacturing; continued faith in the export of primary products; considerable dependence on private enterprise, which means in fact largely foreign private enterprise; a somewhat pessimistic view of the scope for co-operation with neighbouring countries, perhaps because it is now realized that Kenya has had undue privileges in the past; and no real sign of an intention to change the structure of the economy.[9] Indeed, the limited character of the development strategy is even more explicit in Kenya's own statement, where it is summed up under five headings:[10]

An attack on the two principal limitations on growth, shortages of domestic capital and skilled manpower.
The need to revolutionize agriculture.

D

The development of industry 'as rapidly as opportunities are created', with processing of agricultural, livestock, and forestry products.
The expansion of infrastructure 'in order to draw the entire nation into the market economy'.
More equitable distribution.

This statement expounds at some length the need for a mixed economy in terms which are on the face of it lucid and sensible. But in actual practice recent events seem to suggest an increasing reliance on foreign private enterprise and little which can reasonably be called mixed.

To complete the picture, some of the growth targets can be given. Agriculture accounted for 42·3 per cent of domestic output in 1962 and is planned to be 41·4 per cent in 1970. Industry accounted for 24·6 per cent in 1962 and is planned to be 24·1 per cent in 1970. The growth rate of GDP is planned to be 5·2 per cent. It is evident that no structural transformation is envisaged in the present decade, and the contrast with the intentions, at least, of the Tanzanian and Ugandan Governments is also apparent.

A recent comment runs: 'Over the period of the plan, the structure of the Kenyan economy is not to be changed very much. Kenya is not aiming for a radical reconstruction at present. The continuing predominance of agriculture and the lack of emphasis on industrial expansion is surprising, even though in Kenya the industrial sector is relatively well endowed and diversified.'[11]

The *Cameroon* has more industry than other former French territories in Central Africa, concentrated primarily round the port of Douala and to a lesser extent the capital of the country, Yaounde. The population is about 5 million and the physical and human infrastructure is already sufficiently developed for Douala to be a potential growth point of importance. The industries installed include a wide range of food processing, forest industries, and some textiles, and a relatively significant range of metal products, including light steel structures, wire products, sheet working, containers, household utensils, and metal furniture. There are some of the first-stage chemical industries, including sulphuric acid, liquid air, paints, perfumes, and insecticides. Small ships and bicycles are assembled. Thus intermediate goods are only starting and capital goods virtually non-existent.

The exports are agricultural—coffee, cocoa, palm oil, rubber, cotton—with one important exception, aluminium, the Cameroon being at present the only producer of aluminium metal on the African continent. It is primarily for export, although a rolling mill is being installed with, in addition to the domestic market, neighbouring countries in Central Africa and the Ivory Coast in view.

A five-year plan was established covering the period 1961–65 with, as a primary objective, the making of a national state from the former French Cameroon and the former British Southern Cameroon. Much of the Cameroon's problems lie in the field of administration at all levels and the lack of trained personnel, which was given considerable attention in the first plan. This also put much emphasis on the physical infrastructure and on the extension of production of traditional agricultural commodities for export. Industrialization was given a relatively low priority, with the emphasis on facilitating foreign private enterprise.

In the main, progress in the carrying out of the plan was not up to expectation, partly owing to stagnation in the rural sector and partly owing to over-expenditure on social investment. The rate of investment is also relatively low. Good progress has however been made in education and in developing infrastructure.[12]

The second five-year plan for the Cameroon continues to rely on attracting foreign enterprise and on import substitution, mainly of consumer goods. Considerable industrial investment is envisaged, 40 per cent for the development of existing enterprises and the remainder for new industry. A cement works is to be installed in the north, to serve also Chad, and clinker grinding near Douala. The textile industry will continue to expand, as can also be expected of the metal products industry in the Douala area. There will be more highly processed food products, together with plywood, veneers, sacks, and glass bottles. Further development of forest industries, including paper, increased production of aluminium metal, and assembly of electrical apparatus are envisaged as a longer-term project. There are not as yet any signs of serious intentions in the direction of heavy industry, chemicals, and machinery, which would require close co-operation with neighbouring countries in Central Africa. Within such a perspective, as will be seen later, the Cameroon is comparatively well placed.

*Morocco* is a relatively large country with a population of more than 13 million and, by African standards, well developed, with a considerable range of industry established before independence including a wide range of food industry, some forest industries including pulp and paper and packaging, a variety of textiles and allied industries, most building materials, phosphate fertilizer directed to the world market, the beginnings of a significant chemical industry, a wide range of metal products and some electrical equipment, as well as the assembly of transport equipment. On the other hand, there is as yet no heavy industry and little in the way of capital goods.

The first five-year plan, covering the period 1960–64, was intended to make possible considerable advances in industrialization. In fact, the rate of growth of both GDP and manufacturing was disappointing. The intention of the Moroccan authorities was evidently to lay down industries capable of changing the structure of the economy, in addition to developing production of food and other consumer goods, e.g. iron and steel, basic chemicals, and mechanical equipment. It will be seen later how the UAR has made considerable progress in this direction, and it has been pointed out by Samir Amin that there was a marked similarity between the Moroccan and Egyptian plans covering this period.[13] The writer goes on to suggest that the relative lack of success of Morocco has been due to two major factors: the much smaller market in this country and the fact that Egypt's industrialization has been directed essentially by the State, whereas Morocco has relied on domestic and foreign private enterprise. The second factor is in part a reflection of the fact that there has been relatively little change in the basic social structure of Morocco. The first problem can be resolved within the framework of close co-operation in the Maghreb, and this point will be discussed later. There can be no doubt that the strategy of industrial development envisaged by the Moroccan authorities in their first plan remains valid.

*Ethiopia*, in population, is the third largest country in Africa. It has also a very large area and is still, apart from air transport, relatively cut off from neighbouring African countries. Its GDP per head, US $40, is still among the lowest in Africa and the rate of growth of GNP is less than 4 per cent.

Ethiopia has been for all practical purposes independent throughout recorded history and there are now clear signs that this has been an advantage in that, although slowly, it is beginning to make steady progress and that its leaders have the spirit of independence. On the other hand, it also remains true that agricultural development, which is bound to be the main key to general progress for some time to come, is hampered by a prevailing system of land tenure and landlord–farmer relationships which provide limited incentives to peasant farmers to increase production. So far, little progress has been made with land reform, and this is a problem which is more important in Ethiopia than in any other African country. The agricultural potential is immense, and in this above all African countries, industrial development has to be linked with agricultural improvements. This is particularly true of livestock, which could be a major factor for national and sub-regional markets but also for export overseas: meat, processed meat, and related industries, which obviously require modern methods in feeding, veterinary services, and marketing.

Ethiopia remains something of a paradox. The standard indicators of human development in terms of education and training, together with the remnants of a feudal system, would seem generally to be negative. On the other hand, the fact that Ethiopia has avoided colonization means that at the top level, and despite obvious deficiencies in the administrative structure, there are increasing indications not only of a will but also of a competence to develop.[14]

Industrial output is still very limited in relation to total GDP—less than 2 per cent—but it is growing at a rate of about 1·3 per cent per annum. The range of industries established is relatively wide, but this must be judged within the framework of a comparatively large population. In the food industries, apart from the key exports—coffee, oil seeds, and hides and skins—the country is already self-sufficient in sugar and has substantial flour milling, meat, processed milk and dairy products, together with such normal first-stage industries as beer, soft drinks, and the tobacco industries. It is also almost self-sufficient in textiles, other than synthetics. The basic strategy has been import substitution of consumer goods. Intermediate goods are relatively under-developed: cement and other building materials and some first-stage chemicals, some metal products, including scrap-melting and re-rolling. There is a virtual void in capital goods.

So far there have been two five-year plans, the second being due to terminate in 1968. The first plan was concerned mainly with infrastructure and was not entirely fulfilled, owing largely to over-importation of consumer goods.[15] The second plan puts more emphasis on industry, though still relatively little on agriculture, and the GDP targeted growth of 4·6 per cent is still rather low. The industrial strategy is still largely based on import substitution of consumer goods through measures to attract foreign enterprise.

The scope for agricultural industries in Ethiopia is considerable and although progress is being made, more could be done. Reference has already been made to the meat industry and its derivatives. The development of the Awash Valley can also give rise to new industries (apart from cotton and sugar cane, already being exploited) including fruit and vegetables.

Ethiopia is handicapped by insufficient knowledge of its mineral resources. However, it is expected that large-scale production of potash for export will be under way by the end of the sixties. Lack of this kind of information hampers an industrial development strategy in Ethiopia designed to transform the structure of the economy.

Although Ethiopia in population at least is, in contrast to most African countries, large enough to generate substantial industrial development on a national scale, it can gain from co-operation with its neighbours both to the north and to the south. This, however, depends on an improvement in communications, where, rightly, much emphasis has been placed and where significant progress has been made.

*Nigeria* is the most populous country in Africa, with about 55 million, and although incomes per head are low, and although in addition it stands to gain by co-operation with its neighbours, like all African countries, it is large enough to make possible extensive economic development on a national scale, assuming of course that no regions secede.

There is already a wide range of industry, particularly food and forestry products, a wide range of textiles and allied industries, cement and other building materials, a number of first-stage chemicals, and a fair range of metal products. Transport equipment also is assembled.

The first Nigerian plan covers the period 1962–68. Since it was based on the regional plans, it is not really a unified national plan. The main features are development of traditional agricultural commodities for export; dependence on private enterprise mainly but not wholly foreign; expansion of infrastructure; and no serious conception of the structural change of the economy.

The public expenditure envisaged in the plan, valid at current prices, is of the order of Nigerian £830 million, of which so far, in three years, only some £235 million has been carried through. It is obvious, therefore, that the plan cannot be fulfilled. Yet the growth rate of GDP assumed, 4 per cent, was not ambitious. The reasons are partly a relatively low rate of investment and partly a failure to hold down public expenditure on administration, excessive expenditure on social welfare investment, and slow and inadequate project preparation.[16] The main achievements have been in the infrastructural field, the Kainji Dam, transport (including ports), and an oil refinery. There have also been some significant industrial achievements in textiles, cement, rubber manufactures, simple metal goods, and food processing. The time is clearly ripe when Nigeria should proceed from easy import substitution to intermediate products and capital goods. Plans for the production of iron and steel have been hanging fire for some time. It would now be possible to move on from assembly and the simpler metal products to a wide range of metal manufactures, including mechanical and electrical engineering. The production of oil is exceeding expectations, but the associated natural gas is not being used and could be the basis for a substantial basic chemical industry, partly for domestic markets and partly for export, including to African neighbours, e.g. ammonia and nitrogen fertilizer, polyethylene, and viscose rayon.

Active preparations are in hand for the next development plan. It is apparently envisaged that the growth rate of GDP will be raised to 6 per cent, this in turn implying a still higher rate of growth of industry. On the other hand, it is as yet far from clear whether the type of industry envisaged will be along the lines indicated above, designed to change the structure of the economy. It is disappointing to learn that the primary emphasis still seems to be on import substitution and on industries employing low capital output ratios and 'intermediate technology' as ends in themselves.[17]

*Senegal* (and Dakar in particular) was the centre of the former French empire in West Africa. This had the original advantage, for a small country with a population of about 3·5 million, of providing some impetus to industrialization, with the markets of other territories in view; and has the present disadvantage that

Dakar bears some resemblance to Vienna after the First World War, a capital largely cut off from its hinterland.

The country remains predominantly agricultural and, in the case of Dakar, commercial, largely due to its importance as an exporter of groundnut oil and groundnuts to, until recently, an assured market. It has a relatively high GDP, US $190 per head.

Industrialization began relatively early (1920), based in the first instance on the manufacture of oil from groundnuts, and secondly, on industries for local consumption, partly from local raw materials and partly from imported raw materials or semi-finished products. There is a major concentration of industry in Cap Vert and particularly in the area from Dakar to Rufisque.[18] The main industries now installed are food processing, oil, preservation of meat and vegetables, flour and biscuits, and beverages. Other industries are tobacco, textiles, shoes, wood industries, packaging, building materials, simple metal products, first-stage chemicals, and repair and assembly of transport equipment. These industries are almost exclusively French- or Lebanese-owned. As has been pointed out, the starting-point was in the 1920s. The period of rapid expansion was from 1956 to 1959, when the rate of growth of industry was 25 per cent per annum. Subsequently the growth rate has fallen (excluding building) to 17 per cent from 1959 to 1960, 11 per cent from 1960 to 1961, and 1·7 per cent from 1961 to 1962, with subsequently virtual stagnation.

The ISEA study already cited assesses, on the basis of interstructural analysis, how far Cap Vert can be regarded as a genuine growth point and reaches important conclusions.[19] The industries of Cap Vert sell to or buy from each other a very small fraction of their output. Thus the accumulation of industries in a small area is a random collection rather than a coherent complex.

The groundnut oil industry is essentially a point of transit between the main agricultural crop and the French market. Industries catering for the domestic market show a relatively low value added. They are consumer goods industries, inherently not of the kind to promote linkage effects. Cap Vert, in fact, provides only part of the external economies associated with a growth point: a large urban centre, educational facilities, and public services.

The first national plan, from 1961 to 1965, provided for a growth rate of 8 per cent, which in fact turned out to be only 2 per cent.

The next plan, from 1965 to 1969, provides for an increase in the share of agriculture which is in itself perfectly reasonable in view of the need to promote food production for the domestic market; a reduced share of industry, mining, and commerce; an approximately similar share of transport and communications, and some reduction of the high share for social welfare and administration. The principal new industrial projects are the bringing into operation of a phosphate fertilizer plant, a sugar refinery, and a textile works. But there are little or no signs of the basic chemical and machinery industries which would be feasible, and are required, to transform the structure of the economy, this necessarily within the framework of co-operation with neighbouring countries, and in particular the Senegal River Basin countries. A further necessary condition of such a transformation is a move forward towards greater control of the essentials of administration and the direction of industry.

The *Ivory Coast* is another small country, with a population of less than 4 million, which was the second principal centre of the former French West African empire and which has now become by far the most dynamic country in French-speaking Africa south of the Sahara. Over the last fifteen years it has known a remarkable growth rate in both agriculture and industry. Between 1950 and 1965 the rate of growth of agriculture has been more than 7 per cent. If the still higher rates of growth in forestry and fishing are excluded, the rate still remains 6 per cent, more than 9 per cent for export and 3 per cent for the domestic market. This is an experience unparalleled in Africa. The growth rates are even higher in industry—over the whole period 1950–65, 18 per cent, and from 1960 to 1965, 25 per cent.[20]

Until very recently the Ivory Coast has not had a development plan, even in the sense, however limited, of most other African countries, and its industrial achievements are manifestly the result of stable government and measures to attract largely foreign private enterprise. The question, therefore, is how far this boom is likely to continue and in what direction.

The industries now installed fall into three categories: the working up of agricultural products for export (sawn wood, canned tunny fish, canned pineapple, soluble coffee, cocoa-butter, and palm oil); light industries based on local agriculture, metals, textiles, cigarettes, and soap; and, more important for the domestic market, industries based largely on imported raw materials, such as flour milling, light metal products, assembly, and first-stage chemicals. The continued growth of these industries depends on the further growth of agricultural production, the rate of which must inevitably taper off; and on imports of raw materials or semi-finished products, which, together with necessary imports of equipment goods and spare parts, as well as transfer to profits and savings of foreign personnel, weigh heavily on the balance of payments. Furthermore, the limited size of the domestic market means that, as in other countries, the easy stage of import substitution will soon be reached. The striking performance in the Ivory Coast compared, for example, with Senegal, Ghana, and the Democratic Republic of the Congo, simply means that the latter countries have already reached the stage where the growth of this type of industrialization is blocked, whereas the Ivory Coast, starting in 1950 from a much lower level, has been rapidly catching up. It is estimated that the Ivory Coast will have caught up with Senegal in another five years and Ghana in a not much more remote period, unless, of course, there are radical changes in the approach in these two countries.

The Chamber of Commerce in the Ivory Coast has worked out perspectives for the next ten years. The principal projects envisaged are further development of food oil, sugar, biscuits and flour-paste (i.e. spaghetti, etc.), rice, small-scale meat canning; further development of canning of tunny fish and of pineapple, as well as jam and tomatoes, milk products; further extension of the tobacco industry, cotton ginning; further extension of the forestry industries—for both domestic markets and export and including a 170,000 tons cellulose project, mainly for export; extension of textiles and related industries to cover virtually the entire domestic market; further extension of simple metal products and of assembly of passenger vehicles; further extension of plastics manufactures on the basis of imported powder; further extension of simple chemical products, cement and other building materials. Samir Amin puts it:

As can be seen, this assortment of projects is perfectly in line with the strategy of the last fifteen years, on light industry and import substitution, with basic industry excluded. It is to be feared, therefore, that the effect of this choice on the balance of payments may not be more effective than has been seen so often and that when the Ivory Coast has closed the gap with more advanced West African countries (Senegal and Ghana), it will also reach a ceiling and for the same reasons.[21]

Once again, the strategy required is the establishment of basic industries, for which there are obvious possibilities in the Ivory Coast, particularly basic chemicals and metal manufactures, including mechanical and electrical engineering. This also means close co-operation with neighbouring countries in working out a co-ordinated scheme of industrial development. Samir Amin characterizes the Ivory Coast experience as 'growth without development'. He also draws attention to another major factor standing in the way of a movement towards a different strategy, the virtual total dependence of the economy on expatriates. As he points out, it was open to the 'Ivoiriens' in the 1950s to invest in real estate and taxi-cabs. The same is true today and, if the strategy of the Chamber of Commerce is followed, it will be almost as true in 1975.

The *Democratic Republic of the Congo* has a population of more than 15 million, the fourth largest in Africa, but it is thinly populated, since its territory is vast. Industrialization has a comparatively long history and in the final period of Belgian colonization was extremely rapid. Taking 1933–35 as 100, the index of industrial production increased to 615 in 1950. Taking 1950 as 100, it increased to 235 by 1959.[22]

The coverage of industry in the Democratic Republic of the Congo is considerable: virtually all the main food industries; a wide range of textiles and allied products, including rayon, weaving, wool, and synthetics; a wide range of building materials, including an output of cement well beyond the present domestic market, and also asbestos-cement; and a wider range of chemicals than in other African countries south of the Sahara, including sulphuric acid, liquid air, explosives, paints, perfumes, soap, and pesticides; all the main non-ferrous metals, although admittedly for export; a wide range of the simpler metal products; some electrical goods, mainly based on durable consumer goods; and shipbuilding. There has been some approach towards intermediate goods, but capital goods are hardly represented.

Industry has evolved in the Congo in response to two quite different stimuli.[23] One sector, which of its very nature is not homogeneous, has grown in response to overseas export demand:

palm and palm-kernel oil, timber products, and the metallurgical treatment of minerals. With the exception of plywood and veneers, processing does not go beyond the first stage on the basis of the economic interest of the buyers. The other sector, about equal in size, caters for the domestic market and to a limited extent for those of neighbouring countries and is essentially made up of consumer goods. The first wave of industrial investment began in the early twenties and was interrupted by the world depression. The second began in 1950 and petered out about 1958. The main reason was that imports of intermediate and capital goods rose steadily as a result of industrialization and exceeded the capacity to import, based almost entirely on export of primary products. The third was associated with the immediate post-independence years and the accompanying inflation. For a period of twenty years the rate of industrial growth was 14 per cent a year, one of the highest observed anywhere over so long a period. It is not surprising, therefore, that, whether measured by share in GDP or number of industrial workers, the Congo is one of the most industrialized countries in Africa.

The Congolese Government have now stated their intention to prepare a five-year plan, the first of a series which is scheduled to come into force at the beginning of 1968. The strategy to be adopted represents a marked advance on the past. It is based on a recognition that the phase of easy import substitution of consumer goods is largely past, that the time has come to rely primarily on development of the internal market, and, therefore, that much attention must now be paid to the production of intermediate and capital goods. There are twin pillars: the harnessing of the first stage of the Inga power project and the establishment of basic industry supplied therefrom; and the revival of commercial agriculture, but with much more accent on production for the domestic market—manioc, maize, rice, sugar, fish, vegetables, as well as agricultural raw materials for industry—rather than palm and palm-kernel oil, cotton, and rubber for export.

A study prepared as background orientation at the request of the High Commissioner for the Plan defines the alternative approaches.[24] Implicitly, the thesis (which still has some foreign defenders) that the Congo's future lies in continuing to rely on primary products for export overseas is rejected. Explicitly, the study shows three alternative methods—in theory at least—of achieving a 5 per cent GDP growth rate over the period 1963–77. In the first, industry would grow at 7·9 per cent, construction at 7·6 per cent, mining at 3 per cent, and commercial agriculture at 6·4 per cent (which would have to rise to 12·8 per cent in the second plan). Such a high agricultural growth rate is regarded as impossible, so that in practice the growth of GDP would be bound to be less than 5 per cent. The second alternative assumes a growth rate of industry and construction each of 11 per cent, mining 3·7 per cent, and commercial agriculture 3·3 per cent. The third alternative is a minor variant of the second and assumes slightly lower rates for industry and construction and a slightly higher rate for agriculture. It is the second variant which is advocated and this advice has been accepted by the Government.

The study goes on to set out a series of projects prepared for the EEC industrial diversification programme. Taking into account also the basic industry programme associated with Inga, it can be expected that as a minimum the following industries will be installed in the next decade: iron and steel, iron founding, welded tubes, nitrogen fertilizer, caustic soda/chlorine, DDT, PVC, springs, pumps, insulated wire, electric motors and transformers, window glass and bottles, ceramics, paper and cardboard, motor-vehicle tyres, and a considerable range of new food industries. It should be added that, although the domestic Congolese market is the main target and the country is less dependent on the markets of neighbours than most other African countries, it would still benefit from sub-regional co-operation.[25]

*Ghana* is another small country in West Africa, with a population of 7 million, and was the first of the British African colonies to achieve independence. It has a relatively high GDP per head, US $200, a major factor having been the predominance of this country in the world cocoa market. From the outset Ghana has been planning and has set ambitious targets, particularly in the field of education, where much progress has been made, and also in physical infrastructure. Relatively well endowed at independence with transport and communications, including ports, further improvements have been made since independence. A major development has been, of course, the Akosombo Dam, on the Volta River. The energy derived therefrom has now been harnessed, much of which will be taken up by an aluminium smelter under construction; but in addition to meeting the needs of the country

for many years to come, there is a surplus available for neighbouring countries. The range of industry already installed is quite considerable, including a number of food and forest industries, textiles, building materials, scrap melting and re-rolling, and some
metal products.

The development plan covers the period 1963/64 to 1969/70 and
is fairly ambitious in character. The main strategy is similar to that
of Tanzania.[26] On the other hand it has also been pointed out that,
given the general political and social objectives of the Government,
the strategy, at least as far as industrial transformation is concerned, is comparatively timid.[27] Positive factors are the availability of qualified Ghanaians at several levels (and indeed it may
be argued that too great an effort relative to resources is being
made at the level of primary education); a well-developed physical infrastructure; and a high rate of investment, almost 20 per
cent of GDP. To this could have been added the strong foreign
exchange position when independence was achieved, but in fact
this has been subsequently dissipated. In retrospect, it may be seen
that Ghana has had a relatively dynamic approach to formulating
and implementing the progress of rapid economic development;
that it has had an overall conception of development planning,
with execution based on both public and private enterprise; and
that the Government had at least considerable mass understanding and support.[28]

It should, of course, be remembered that the drastic fall in cocoa
prices was not something which could have been wholly foreseen,
and this naturally falsified a number of early expectations. Yet
also in retrospect it can be seen that there have been two major
weaknesses. The first became evident with the 1966 change of
government, the neglect of elementary economic principles, trying
to do too much at once, and a degeneration into something approaching economic chaos; the second and more fundamental
point is (as in other African countries) the lack of a real strategy
of industrial development concerned to manufacture intermediate
and capital goods, this in turn requiring close co-operation with
neighbouring countries. The former Government of Ghana pro-
claimed the ideal of all-African co-operation, but in practice was
somewhat unrealistic in its attitude and little concerned with practical co-operation with its neighbours.

The two countries in the last group adopted earlier in this chapter have now been reached—those which have not only a coherent strategy of industrial development but have also made some real progress: Tunisia and the UAR.

*Tunisia* is a small country with a population of about 4 million. In the 1950s the growth rate of GDP was 3·5 per cent, on the basis of an already fairly well developed agricultural sector oriented towards European markets and a significant range of industry. The growth rate rose to 6 per cent from 1960 to 1964, the last three years being covered by the first development plan. Investment was high and the marginal domestic savings rate 20 per cent. The long-term capital inflow rose to 12 per cent by 1964, but was short of expectations. The 1965–68 plan assumes the same growth rate as in the previous five years and an investment ratio of 23 per cent of GDP. It is hoped to raise the marginal savings rate to 35 per cent.

The present range of industry is considerable. In addition to an important mining sector, there are a wide range of food industries; textiles and clothing; a significant basic chemical sector based on production of phosphate fertilizers; metal products; paper and packaging; shoes and leather goods; forest industries; non-metallic minerals; and rubber manufactures.[29] An iron and steel works is now in production with a target of 80,000 tons of rolled products by 1968, although admittedly at a high investment cost per ton owing to the small scale of output (US $515 per ton).

So far the forward linkages from domestically produced manufactured goods have been comparatively limited, but the value of these manufactures derived from imports is relatively low, 20 to 25 per cent.

The second development plan assumes an industrial growth rate of 15·3 per cent. The significant features are the steady expansion of phosphate fertilizers involving also production of ammonia (derived from naphtha from the refinery), ammonium sulphate, phosphoric acid, sulphuric acid, die-ammonium phosphate, and ammonium nitrate. Building materials are well represented, with a target of 630,000 tons of cement.

Vans, small trucks, and buses are being assembled, again at an uneconomic scale of output, based largely on the Menzel–Bourguiba complex. A significant start has been made in the field of engineering, including metal working, spare parts for mechanical engineering, diesel engineering assembly, the manufacture of looms, tractor assembly, and household equipment.

Tunisia has established not only a coherent development plan but also serious arrangements for the execution of its plan, based admittedly on a much higher proportion of trained personnel at all levels than in most African countries. There is also a major State sector, both in terms of investment and execution of industrial enterprises, not, in the Government's view, owing to any doctrinaire preoccupations or hostility to private enterprise, but of necessity.

The Tunisian progress towards changing the structure of its economy is one of the most encouraging features of the present African scene, but it is bound to be checked unless larger markets can be found, primarily through intimate co-operation at the level of the Maghreb.

The *United Arab Republic* is by far the most industrialized country in Africa. It has the advantage of a relatively large population, about 30 million. It is true, of course, that the income per head is still relatively low. The UAR has therefore been able to plan its development programme within the framework of its own national market. It could gain from co-operation with its neighbours, but has so far shown little interest in so doing.

This short sketch cannot, of course, do justice to the development policies of this country. Suffice for present purposes to indicate in broad outline what has been achieved. The geographical area of the UAR is not extensive and the population pressure is greater than in many African countries. Despite intensive agriculture in terms of inputs, particularly irrigation and fertilizers, agriculture remains a constraint on development, with the normal pressures on the balance of payments as economic development proceeds.

There is the whole range of food industries, apart, of course, from tropical products, and some forest industries. Textiles are strongly represented in all branches both for the domestic market and for export. The whole range of building materials is produced. Iron and steel is produced from domestic raw materials, admittedly at high cost, and also some non-ferrous metals. It is planned to produce aluminium in the near future. There is a basic chemical industry. The normal range of metal products is manufactured. In the mechanical engineering field, internal combustion engines, agricultural machinery, vertical drilling machines, saws for metal and wood working, grinding machines, weighing machines, winches and hoisting equipment, sewing machines, and valves and light pumps are all produced. There is a wide range of electrical machinery, including motors, transformers, switch gear, insulated cables and wire insulators, welding electrodes, as well as durable consumer goods such as electric irons, stoves, refrigerators, lamp bulbs and tubes, transistor radios, and television sets. Transport equipment is being assembled and there is progressive manufacture of components.

The foundations of modern industry were laid in the thirties, but the real impetus to development came with the 1952 revolution. It has been estimated that the annual rate of increase of manufacturing industry from 1951 to 1962 was about 7 to 8 per cent, approximately twice that of GNP.

The policies underlying industrial development have been summarized in a recent study.[30] First, import duties were reduced on machinery and raw materials not available locally, but sharply increased on most other commodities, reinforced by import licensing. Secondly, financial incentives have been given to industries considered likely to promote national economic development. Thirdly, industrial development has been not only fostered by the Government but also planned through an economic development organization set up in 1957, empowered to enter directly into industrial production. Fourthly, steps have been taken not only to promote national saving but also to direct savings into industrial development. Fifthly, money wages have been held down by controlling at a low level prices of essential consumer goods and by assistance under US Public Law 480.

The rate of increase of manufacturing output accelerated from 1957 to such an extent that by 1960 the share of manufacturing in GDP rose by one-third. A major element has been, of course, the growth of import substitution industries under protection, to the extent that further possibilities in the field of consumer goods are now limited. At the same time there has been a rapid development of basic metals and engineering. It has proved possible to develop export of manufactures, particularly textiles, and also cement, chemical and pharmaceutical products, paper and paper products, and rubber manufactures.

It is clear from the foregoing that the UAR has already moved into the stage of production of intermediate and capital goods, primarily designed to transform the structure of the economy, but also towards the beginning of export of manufactures.

E

# NOTES AND REFERENCES TO CHAPTER II

[1] Data have been drawn from many sources, including country reports prepared by governments for the African Industrial Symposium held in Cairo in 1966; official government reports from Ethiopia, Morocco, Algeria, Sudan, Uganda, Kenya, and Nigeria; *Bulletin de l'Afrique Noire, Europe France Outre-Mer*, and *Industries et travaux d'outre-mer*.

[2] The details of each development plan are not given here. See, apart from the texts of the plans themselves, *Outlines and Selected Indicators of African Development Plans*, UN ECA (document E/CN. 14/336), Addis Ababa, 1965.

[3] G. Bell, '*Le projet de pôle électro-métallurgique de FRIA*', *Cahiers de l'ISEA*, September 1963.

[4] Samir Amin, *Trois expériences africaines de développement: le Mali, la Guinée et le Ghana*, Paris, 1965, p. 162.

[5] Samir Amin comments on the failure in this respect in Mali and Guinea, but what he says is applicable to most African countries. He shows that Mali and Guinea have placed emphasis on village co-operatives, not only for trading and obtaining supplies but also for collective cultivation and administrative and technical services, including the technical education of the peasants. The approach derives essentially from the last years of French colonialization and is applied throughout French Africa, despite widely differing political outlooks. He states, however, 'What must be done to make progress in agriculture is not to "educate the peasants within the traditional framework of the family but to break down the family and its traditions". Neither is it by the setting up of illusory and formal co-operatives but by harnessing individual enterprise and liberating the individual from the stranglehold of tradition' (Samir Amin, ibid., p. 231).

[6] R. H. Green, 'Four African Development Plans', *Journal of Modern African Studies*, Vol. 3, No. 2, 1965, p. 264.

[7] R. H. Green, 'Ugandans Prepare to Work for Progress', *East African Journal*, August 1966.

[8] Paul Clark, 'Development Strategy in an Early Stage Economy: Uganda', *Journal of Modern African Studies*, Vol. 4, No. 1, 1966.

[9] R. H. Green, 'Four African Development Plans', op. cit., p. 265.

[10] Republic of Kenya, *African Socialism and Its Application to Planning in Kenya*, 1965, p. 28.

[11] Judith Hyer, 'Kenya's Cautious Development Plan', *East African Journal*, August 1966.

[12] See *Report of the ECA Mission on Economic Co-operation in Central Africa*, United Nations (Sales No. 66. K.11), New York, 1966.

[13] Samir Amin, *L'Économie du Maghreb: les perspectives d'avenir*, Éditions de Minuit, Paris, pp. 117–18.

[14] See in this context Richard Pankhurst, 'Ethiopia: A Case Study in Independent African Development', paper contributed to the Haile Selassie I Prize Trust Foundation Seminar, Addis Ababa, October 1966.

[15] In this brief account of the situation in Ethiopia an unpublished note by Hans Singer has been drawn upon, and also a study by Krishna Ahooja, to be published, on *Investment Laws in Ethiopia*.

[16] For an analysis of the Nigerian plan and its weaknesses, in both conception and execution, see R. H. Green, 'Four African Development Plans', op. cit.

[17] See *Guideposts for the Second National Development Plan*, Ministry of Economic Development, Lagos, 1966.

[18] Much of the data in this section is drawn from *Les Industries du Cap Vert*, ISEA, Dakar, 1964.

[19] Ibid., p. 74.

[20] Samir Amin, *Le Développement économique et social de la Côte d'Ivoire*, IDEP, Dakar, 1966.

[21] Samir Amin, ibid, p. 329.

[22] J. L. Lacroix: '*Les pôles de développement industriel dans le Congo*', *Cahiers économiques et sociaux*, Université Lovanium, Kinshasa, Cahier No. 2, October 1964.

[23] See J. L. Lacroix, *Industrialisation au Congo: la transformation des structures économiques*, op. cit.

[24] *Étude d'orientation pour le plan de développement et de diversification industrielle*, IRES, Université Lovanium, Kinshasa, July 1966.

[25] See *Report of the ECA Mission on Economic Co-operation in Central Africa*, op. cit., Chap. VIII.

[26] See R. H. Green, 'Four African Development Plans', op. cit.

[27] Samir Amin, *Trois expériences africaines de développement*, op. cit., pp. 193–206.

[28] R. H. Green, 'Four African Development Plans', op. cit., pp. 275–6.

[29] See R. Genoud, *Évolution de l'économie tunisienne*, Geneva, 1965; and Samir Amin, *L'Économie du Maghreb: les perspectives d'avenir*, op. cit., pp. 47 ff.

[30] B. Hansen and G. A. Marzouk, *Development and Economic Policy in the UAR*, Amsterdam, 1965.

# CHAPTER III

# SOME NOTES ON INDUSTRIAL GROWTH OUTSIDE AFRICA

The first two chapters have suggested the role of industry in industrial development and have shown the degree of industrialization in Africa at present, based on what exists, how it has evolved in recent years, and what are the intentions of the governments concerned.

This chapter examines briefly the experience of other selected developing countries. The countries concerned have made more progress than most African countries and most of them have a significantly higher GDP per head. They are also, almost without exception, much larger than all but two or three African countries in population, an advantage which is open to African countries only if they group their economies.

On the whole, the experience of Asia is of limited significance for Africa at the present time. It is not a homogeneous continent, with the whole spectrum in terms of both stage and level of development. Economic integration is of less significance than in Africa and in any case there has been little practical experience. A brief reference will be made, however, to the relevant experience of Japan and Israel in development.

Japan and Israel are two economies which have grown rapidly over the last decade, at more than 10 per cent a year. Part of the explanation lies in the availability of a strong skilled labour force and ample entrepreneurial skills—but these explanations are not sufficient. Japan invested at a rate of 39 per cent of GNP in the first five years of the decade, rising to 44 per cent of GNP in 1961. Israel's investment rate was about 30 per cent of GNP between 1960 and 1963. In the case of Japan, net capital imports were fairly small, but they were 50 per cent of total investment in the case of Israel. Both countries maintained low capital output ratios, between 2 and 3. Both countries make extensive use of small-scale industry, Israel more than Japan, but it should be remembered that this is largely possible owing to the ability to apply large amounts of highly skilled labour to inexpensive machinery. Both countries have relatively new capital stock and a flexible policy of shifting capital in directions where the growth of labour productivity is high. Private savings are largely mobilized through the commercial banking mechanism and there is no broadly based capital market.[1]

There are other features of particular interest to developing countries in the Japanese experience. Thus, the economy remains a dual one with co-existence between labour-intensive agriculture and small-scale industries on the one hand, and highly capital-intensive industries on the other. Despite the density of population, there is no over-population, owing to the level of education and degree of training of the labour force. Agriculture is necessarily highly intensive, owing to the limited area of the country. Raw material endowment is limited, and this has stimulated constant application of technology to economize in materials.

The limited time scale of Japanese development is also of major interest. In 1910, per capita income was US $110.00 at 1951 prices, not far off the present average for Africa. In the next twenty-five years, industrial development really got under way. During this period changes in the structure of production were due almost entirely to domestic and foreign demand, with a competitive exporting sector and a relatively limited import substitution. In the following twenty years, difficulties in exporting began to appear and it was then that import substitution and technological change became important.

The third period, beginning in 1955, shows major structural changes, at which period heavy industry accounted for 50 per cent of total industrial output and there began to be greater emphasis on export of heavy machinery. By 1960, 41 per cent of Japanese exports were heavy industrial products, and 37 per cent were from light industry. By 1970 it is estimated that 73 per cent of total industrial output will be heavy industry.[2]

The twenty Latin American countries can be divided into three groups, on the basis of approximate real annual income per head.[3] The top six have incomes per head varying from US $780 in Argentina to US $420 in Panama, and include also Venezuela, Uruguay, Chile, and Mexico. The middle three have incomes varying from US $390 (Brazil, Colombia) to US $350 (Costa Rica). The poorest ten have incomes varying from US $320 (Nicaragua) to US $120 (Haiti) and also include the Dominican Republic,

Peru, El Salvador, Guatemala, Honduras, Ecuador, Paraguay, and Bolivia. Cuba, before the revolution, was also in the top group, but recent data are not available. There are five countries in Latin America with a population of 11 million or more, i.e. Peru (11 million), Colombia (17 million), Argentina (21 million), Mexico (40 million), and Brazil (80 million).

Three of the countries in the top group, Argentina, Uruguay, and Chile, are in the temperate zone and were relatively prosperous before the depression of the thirties. The other three, Venezuela, Mexico, and Panama, are relatively well off owing partly to oil, tourism, and the Canal Zone, respectively.

The middle three countries (Brazil, Colombia, and Costa Rica) are all heavily dependent on the export of coffee. The poorest countries are primarily dependent on one or two agricultural exports, other than Bolivia, which lives on tin. These countries have each of them installed a selection of the usual first-stage import substitution industries.

Since the war there has been a marked change in the structure of production in Latin America as a whole, although evidently there are differences from country to country. The ECLA study referred to analyses the change in the structure of production under four headings: the income level, its distribution and variation; public expenditure; external demand; and the process of import substitution. It points out that the distribution of income in Latin America is very unequal and that greater equalization would have a marked effect on the evolution of production.[4] As to the second factor, public expenditure, it is pointed out that in the last few years this has constituted about 13 per cent of final demand. External demand is a major influence. Thus 90 per cent of mining production in Bolivia, Chile, Mexico, and Peru is exported. Agricultural commodities sold abroad account for about one-third of this sector's total output in Brazil and Colombia and more than three-quarters in Costa Rica, Ecuador, and El Salvador.

Although, as has already been pointed out, import substitution is now diminishing in influence, it has been a major factor. Since the war, production of manufactured consumer goods has been increasing at a rate of 3 to 4 per cent per annum, while that of intermediate or durable goods in which substitution has predominated, including assembly, increased at an annual rate of 10 per cent or more. A quantitative measure of the influence of import substitution has been the fact that during the post-war period the growth rate of imports was only 75 per cent of the domestic product and internal income, and 60 per cent of that of manufacturing output.

Except in two countries, Ecuador and Mexico, the rate of increase of agricultural output has been a constraint on development, the dynamic factors having been industry and building. The primary sector, which accounted for 35 per cent of total domestic product in 1936–40, has fallen to 28 per cent and the share of manufacturing and building has risen from 18 to 24 per cent.

Two factors stand out. One is that the external sector has been a progressively weakening factor in Latin American development, partly because of the inherent difficulty in finding a sufficient rate of growth of markets for primary products and partly because of deterioration in the terms of trade. Thus, it is estimated that from 1955 to 1961 the volume of Latin American exports was 34 per cent greater than in the preceding period, but that their purchasing power rose by only 13 per cent. The second factor is that Latin American development has been essentially externally geared.

In the fifties, the process of import substitution covered consumer goods, building materials, and, to some extent, durable capital goods as well. As far as fuels and intermediate goods are concerned, however, the process was undoubtedly less intensive in relative terms, or else the replacement of some goods was offset by heavier imports of others.[5]

Since, as will be seen later, limited progress has been made in the Latin American free trade area (although somewhat more encouraging in Central America) and thus prospects of expanding the market for intermediate and capital goods by export to each other are for the present limited, it is not surprising that the main emphasis in Latin American policy now is to try to force open the doors of the developed countries to exports of their manufactures.

Argentina is still the richest country in Latin America in terms of real income per head and has also a relatively large population, over 20 million. Forty years ago, before the world depression, it was one of the six or seven richest countries in the world. For all practical purposes it has subsequently stagnated. Some 45 per cent of its exports are meat, wool, and other animal products, and another 25 per cent are grains. Of these commodities only meat is likely to enjoy steadily increasing demand, and Argentina's share of the total world market has fallen heavily. A large part of the problem lies in the fact that although Argentina is well endowed by nature with agricultural resources, it has made little progress in modernizing this sector, e.g. a limited use of fertilizers and low cattle yields. A second difficulty is that the transport system has been allowed to run down. These are perhaps the main priorities and are illustrated, on the other side of the medal, by a low rate of growth of manufacturing industry. Taking 1945–49 as 100, the index for 1950–54 was 106·8 and for 1956–61, 123·7. The corresponding indices for Brazil are 155·0 and 280·8.

A number of points have already been made about Brazil. Its population is twice as much as the second largest country in Latin America, its area is vast, it is well endowed with natural resources, its degree of industrial development is considerable, as has been shown by the figures just quoted and by the way in which import substitution has been pushed right into intermediate and some capital goods.[6] There have been two major difficulties. One is the backwardness of agriculture, with too many people still working on the land and a low rate of growth, partly as a result of the fact that 10 per cent of Brazil's landowners own 80 per cent of the farmland and the other 90 per cent own only 20 per cent, with many more still owning no land at all. The second major problem is that the annual rate of inflation in recent years, over 60 per cent, has been much more than twice as much as in the other Latin American countries where prices are rising rapidly—Argentina, Uruguay, and Chile. Brazil has been the main laboratory of ECLA's 'structuralist' view of inflation compared with the 'monetary' view. It is still a dual economy, where constraints arise in one sector and lead to price rises which are not only cumulative in themselves but give rise to expectations of further increases. In such a situation deflation becomes largely irrelevant.[7]

Mexico is the country in Latin America which has been most successful in the development process, whether measured by rate of growth of real income per head over a long period, by both agricultural and industrial development, or by stabilization of the price level. The Second World War was a significant stimulus, but expansion continued subsequently, promoted by tourism, import substitution, and the inflow of both foreign capital and technical aid. Perhaps still more important, there appears to have been a judicious balance between the role of the State and the emergence of a climate propitious for indigenous private enterprise.[8]

As in other Latin American countries, Mexico's growth has been partly dependent on the external sector, but the country has been fortunate in being able to depend on a considerable range of primary products and has also been able, as time went on, to develop new primary exports. Traditional exports include coffee, fruit, vegetables, cotton, and non-ferrous metals. More recently developing exports include sulphur, cattle, fish, sugar, and tomatoes. The flourishing tourist trade has already been mentioned. In the last few years there have been signs of a slowing down in the rate of growth of the economy and uncertainties about the future, which are part and parcel of the familiar Latin American problem already analysed: the weakening of external stimuli and the end of the easy stage of import substitution. By the early sixties, consumer goods were less than one-fifth of Mexico's total imports. Intermediate goods, such as basic chemicals, artificial fibres, and steel, are now being produced in quantity. But to go farther, particularly to become a large-scale producer of capital goods, means either to find new markets elsewhere in Latin America, or in the developed world, owing to economies of scale. The population is admittedly large, 40 million, and growing rapidly, but only a comparatively small fraction of the economy has a sufficiently large income per head to constitute a large market. It is true that there is theoretically much scope for rectification of the distribution of income, but despite the significant and intelligent role of the State, there is still substantial dependence on both foreign and domestic private enterprise. Hence the dilemma so far as radical measures of redistribution of income are concerned.

The last example taken from Latin America is Peru, a country much closer in characteristics to those in Africa.[9] In 1955 Peru had a per capita income of US $190 and a population of almost 9 million (now over 11 million). Of the population 60 per cent were engaged in agriculture, but generated only 30 per cent of the national income; 2 per cent were employed in manufacturing and generated 17 per cent of the national income. There was a dual economy and strong external dependence. On the other hand, natural resources are abundant and there was a high rate of growth in the decade to 1955, with some structural change. In addition to the need to develop agriculture, the key problem facing the economy in 1955 was industrialization, partly to absorb manpower, given the high rate of population growth, and partly to substitute imports. The structure of Peruvian industry in 1955 was concentrated largely on food processing, beverages, and textiles. The detailed analysis and projections made by ECLA revealed and worked out development possibilities in a wide range of food industries (particularly fish), paper, leather, rubber, fertilizers, sulphuric acid, a caustic/chlorine complex, pharmaceuticals, synthetic fibres, petroleum and coal derivatives, a wide range of nonmetallic minerals, iron and steel, non-ferrous metals, a wide range of metal products, agricultural machinery, mining machinery, woodworking machinery, some electrical equipment, shipbuilding (with the fishing industry in view), commercial vehicles, and railway equipment. These are illustrations only. The range of metal-based manufactures considered feasible and projected was astonishingly wide for a country at that level of development. While data are not available as to how far these projections have been realized, the subsequent progress of the economy has been encouraging, with a GDP now of over US $300 per head. The expansion of a modern fishing industry has been phenomenal.

This brief sketch of the experience of developing countries is completed by that of one European country, Yugoslavia, which not long ago was under-developed and dependent. The following passage, from an ECA report, which is quoted in full, was prepared within the particular context of showing what could be done to lay down intermediate and capital goods based on metals in Central Africa, in other words, the successful application of the strategy advocated in this study. Yugoslav experience would seem to be relevant to economic areas comparable in Africa.

In 1939 Yugoslavia was a poor under-developed country, with the familiar characteristics. About three-quarters of the population were engaged in agriculture, the key activity was mining for export of non-ferrous metal ores which were processed in the country to only a limited extent. The technical level of such industry as existed was extremely low, with very limited metal working and virtually no production of machinery. The primary sector accounted for about 55 per cent and industry less than 20 per cent of the national income.* The country

---

* For these data and what follows, see *Study of the requirements of European countries in process of industrialization for engineering products: Yugoslavia*, ENG/CONF/Working paper No. 5, ECE, Geneva, March 1965.

suffered severe war damage. During the period 1948–52 the average annual rate increase in the national income was 1·9 per cent. It rose to 8·4 per cent during the period 1953–56 and 12·9 per cent during the period 1957–60. Already by 1956 industry accounted for 44 per cent of the national income and agriculture for 41 per cent. Throughout the ten-year period 1952–63 the average rate of growth of capital investment in mechanical engineering and metal working was extremely high, considerably greater than that for investment in industry as a whole. Total capital investment in industry increased by 200 per cent, capital investment in mechanical engineering by 340 per cent. The share of mechanical engineering as a whole in total capital investment rose to 14·4 per cent in 1963. By 1962 metal working and mechanical engineering accounted for 24·6 per cent of the total value of industrial production.

Table 70 shows the output of selected metal manufacturing industries in Yugoslavia in 1939/1963.

Table 70

OUTPUT OF SELECTED METAL MANUFACTURING INDUSTRY IN YUGOSLAVIA IN 1939 AND 1963

| Type of Industry | Unit of measurement | 1939 | 1963 |
|---|---|---|---|
| Bearings | tons | nil | 1,596 |
| Machine tools | tons | 84 | 6,240 |
| Building materials and equipment | tons | 108 | 7,305 |
| Refrigerating equipment | tons | nil | 860 |
| Internal combustion engines | units | nil | 67,849 (1962) |
| Agricultural machines | tons | 1,805 | 22,207 |
| Tractors | units | nil | 8,092 |
| Lorries | units | nil | 7,975 |
| Light vans | units | nil | 20,923 |
| Buses | units | nil | 1,028 |
| Motor cycles | units | nil | 43,113 |
| Bicycles | 1,000 units | nil | 290 |
| Railway goods wagons | units | nil | 2,762 |
| Electric motors | 1,000 kw | nil | 644 |
| Transformers | 1,000 kva | nil | 2,301 |
| High voltage incandescent lamps | 1,000 units | 2,522 | 21,119 |

*Source: Study of the requirements of European countries in process of industrialization for engineering products: Yugoslavia, op. cit. (extracted from Table 10).*

Metal products have been excluded since although there have been very large increases there was already significant production of a number of items in 1939, this sector being, as already noted, the one in the group which normally starts first. What is striking is the increase in production of key capital goods either from nil or from very low levels.

The population of Yugoslavia in 1939 was approximately 14,500,000 and rose to 18,600,000 in 1963. The gross domestic product rose from US $42 per head in 1945 (when it was certainly not higher than before the war) to US $274 in 1963.* The experience of Yugoslavia gives a pointer to how a country which had in 1939 a population, a GDP per head and structural characteristics not significantly different from the Central African sub-region today, has been able, in a period of effectively less than twenty years, to transform completely its industrial structure and establish a relatively advanced engineering industry.[10]

Although the comparison between the Central African countries as a group and Yugoslavia, and therefore the suggestions as to what could be achieved by the former in the light of the experience of the latter, are perfectly reasonable, an important point has been overlooked. This is that, despite economic backwardness and external domination in 1939, Yugoslavia was already then richer in human material than Central Africa today. This has its own lessons, as will be shown in Chapters VII and VIII. Reference may also usefully be made to a comparison of the performance of Yugoslavia and its neighbours in Southern Europe. This is possible on the basis of an ECE study,[11] which analyses the development performances and problems of Yugoslavia, Greece, Turkey, Spain, Portugal, Southern Italy (and also Ireland). Leaving out Southern Italy, which is a special case because of the fact that it is part of Italy and thus linked to the richer north, Yugoslavia has been the most successful, whether measured by industrial and agricultural growth, the transformation of its economic structure through the laying down of intermediate and capital goods, import substitution and the cutting out of unnecessary imports, export diversification, the promotion of saving, or the raising of the rate of investment. This has been made possible largely by deliberate government policy and the intervention of the State by one means or another in many fields.

* *UN Demographic Yearbook 1962–1963; Growth and Stagnation of the European Economy*, ECE, Geneva, 1954, p. 237; *UN Yearbook of National Account Statistics, 1952* and *1963*.

# NOTES AND REFERENCES TO CHAPTER III

[1] O. W. McDiarmid, 'Japan and Israel', *Finance and Development*, Vol. III, No. 2, Washington, 1966.

[2] *Report of the Seminar on Industrial Programming*, ECLA (document E/CN. 12/663), 1963.

[3] The data in the section on Latin American countries are drawn mainly from two sources: *The Economic Development of Latin America in the Post-war Period*, United Nations (Sales No. 64. II. G.6), New York and 'An Economic Survey of Latin America', *The Economist*, 25 September 1965. See also *The Process of Industrial Development in Latin America*, ECLA (Sales No. 66. II. G.4), New York, 1966.

[4] This problem is discussed fully in Chapter VI.

[5] *The Economic Development of Latin America in the Post-war Period*, op. cit., p. 23.

[6] Baer, *Industrialization and Economic Development in Brazil*, op. cit., Chaps. 3 and 6.

[7] Ibid., Chap. 7.

[8] Here and subsequently in this section, see R. Vernon, *The Dilemma of Mexico's Development*, Harvard, 1963.

[9] The data summarized here are taken from one of the most detailed country studies on industry which have yet been prepared: *The Industrial Development of Peru*, ECLA secretariat, United Nations (Sales No. 59. II. G.2), New York, 1959.

[10] *Report of the ECA Mission on Economic Co-operation in Central Africa*, op. cit., Chap. VII.

[11] See the *Economic Survey of Europe in 1959*, United Nations (Sales No. 60. II. E.1), Geneva, Chaps. VII and VIII.

# CHAPTER IV

# PROSPECTS FOR INDUSTRIAL GROWTH IN AFRICA

This chapter first sets out the outlines of a growth framework for African development based on 1976–80 and, in very broad outline, the end of the century. These figures are quantitative guesswork. What is suggested is feasible, given appropriate policies. No

Table 2

AN OUTLINE OF THE POSSIBLE ECONOMIC DEVELOPMENT OF AFRICA, 1980–2000

| Sector of origin | Net domestic product | | | Structure | | | Annual rate of growth | |
| --- | --- | --- | --- | --- | --- | --- | --- | --- |
| | 1960 | 1980 | 2000 | 1960 | 1980 | 2000 | 1960–1980 | 1980–2000 |
| | (billion US dollars [1960]) | | | (per cent) | | | (per cent) | |
| I Agriculture, etc. | 11 | 30 | 75 | 35 | 30 | 20 | 5·2 | 4·7 |
| II Industry | 6·6 | 30 | 165 | 20 | 30 | 40 | 7·9 | 8·9 |
| Commodity output: total | 18 | 60 | 240 | 55 | 60 | 60 | 6·2 | 7·2 |
| III Other sectors | 14 | 40 | 160 | 45 | 40 | 40 | 5·4 | 7·2 |
| Total product | 32 | 100 | 400 | 100 | 100 | 100 | 5·9 | 7·2 |
| Industry: | 6·6 | 30 | 165 | 20 | 30 | 40 | 7·9 | 8·9 |
| Mining | 2·2 | 7 | 25 | 7 | 7 | 6 | 6·0 | 6·6 |
| Manufacturing: | | | | | | | | |
| Light | 2·9 | 10 | 55 | 9 | 10 | 14 | 6·4 | 8·9 |
| Heavy | 1·5 | 13 | 85 | 5 | 13 | 20 | 11·4 | 9·8 |

*Sources and methods:* Data for 1960 from *United Nations Yearbook of National Accounts Statistics 1961* and *1962*, and national statistics; some of the gaps in the data have been filled in by partial estimates. The estimates for 1980 and 2000 derived on the basis of the growth framework given below. This table is reproduced from A. F. Ewing and S. J. Patel, 'Perspectives for Industrialization in Africa,' *Man and Africa*, London, 1965.

prophecies are intended. It should be obvious that any indications of possible industrial development cannot be of value in isolation from the general movement of the African economy and of the world economy as a whole. The next step is to examine by types of industry what Africa could do. Preliminary studies now available, particularly by the ECA, go into great detail. What is included here is essentially illustrative and has been deliberately selected on the basis of the strategy of industrial development outlined in the first chapter and shown in the second to be sorely needed, if serious advances are to be made. After a discussion of the types of industry, the threads of the argument are drawn together in terms of appropriate economic groupings within Africa, an essential step if real progress is to be contemplated.

As a first step, therefore, the possibilities of development in Africa are shown in outline form. An underlying assumption is steadily increasing economic co-operation among African countries, moving towards economic integration among suitable groupings thereof. The framework is set out in Table 2.

The outline of the growth framework can be seen from Table 3.

Table 3

## THE GROWTH FRAMEWORK
(Total gross domestic product for 1960—100)

| Sector of origin | | 1960 | 1980 | 2000 |
|---|---|---|---|---|
| I | Agriculture | 35 | 95 | 235 |
| II | Industry | 20 | 95 | 515 |
| | Commodity output | 55 | 190 | 750 |
| III | Other sectors | 45 | 125 | 500 |
| | Total product | 100 | 315 | 1,250 |
| IV | Gross capital formation | 13–14 | 63 | 250 |

GDP is assumed to rise from US $32 billion in 1960 to US $100 billion in 1980 and US $400 billion by the year 2000. This requires an annual growth rate of 5·9 per cent for the first period and 7·2 per cent for the second.

Three estimates of population have been employed. The low estimate is 442 million in 1980 and 620 million in 2000. The medium estimate is 457 million in 1980 and 737 million in 2000. The high is 473 million in 1980 and 879 million in 2000. The three assumptions used depend on different hypotheses of fertility and mortality rates. It is difficult at this stage to choose a definite hypothesis, but two important factors should be taken into consideration. First, decline in fertility usually bears a certain relationship to levels of income and education. If the rapid development projects are realized there would seem to be a serious possibility of the decline in fertility setting in much earlier than has hitherto been assumed. Secondly, the progress towards cheaper and more effective methods of birth control may be expected to be rapid. The World Health Organization (WHO) anti-malaria campaign has produced dramatic results and it is not unreasonable to expect that a similar campaign for birth control may be launched before long. If the medium population forecast proves to be correct the level of per capita income will rise from US $115 in 1960 to about US $545 in 2000. On the low assumption it would be US $645. The former is equal to the average in Western Europe in the middle fifties and the latter to that in the late fifties.

The average levels of Western Europe could be achieved even if growth rates were somewhat lower than estimated. This is because the output of agriculture and services is seriously undervalued in less developed countries. This is particularly true so far as African agriculture is concerned though perhaps not to the same extent concerning services, owing to the high share of expatriates in this sector in 1960. It is now widely accepted that if the per capita incomes of the developing countries were to be compared with those in the developed countries they should be raised significantly.[1]

The growth framework adopted suggests a significant transformation of the economic structure of Africa. The share of agriculture would fall from 35 per cent in 1960 to 20 per cent by the end of the century. That of industry would rise from 20 to 40 per cent.

It has been estimated[2] that assuming a 'medium' projection for African population growth, the labour force will rise from 112,124,000 in 1960 to 136,348,000 in 1970, 168,338,000 in 1980, and 279,516,000 in 2000, an increase of two and a half times in the four decades. The additions to the labour force can be absorbed to only a limited extent in industry, from which it follows that to provide anything approaching full employment, sustained efforts are required in the rural sector, agriculture, and physical infrastructure, and in all forms of construction where labour-intensive methods are appropriate.

This in turn shows the importance of a high rate of agricultural growth. The illustrative projections, which, it should be stressed again, are not predictions but indications of desirable and basically attainable targets, are undoubtedly ambitious in the agricultural sector and indeed in the early part of the period unrealistic, since six years have already passed and actual performance has

Table 4

## ESTIMATES OF NET INDUSTRIAL OUTPUT
## IN AFRICA FOR 1960–1980 AND 1980–2000

| Type of industry | Value in billion US dollars (1960 prices) | | | Annual rate of growth (per cent) | |
|---|---|---|---|---|---|
| | 1960* | 1980* | 2000* | 1960–80 | 1980–2000 |
| *Industrial output* | 6·6 | 30 | 165 | 7·9 | 8·9 |
| Mining | 2·2 | 7 | 25 | 6·0 | 6·6 |
| Manufacturing | 4·4 | 23 | 140 | 8·6 | 9·5 |
| *Light industry* | 2·9 | 10·0 | 55·0 | 6·4 | 8·9 |
| Food, beverages, and tobacco | 1·0 | 3·1 | 16·7 | 5·8 | 8·8 |
| Textiles, Clothing, footwear, and made-up textiles | 1·0 | 3·7 | 16·2 | 6·7 | 7·7 |
| Wood products and furniture | ... | 1·2 | 5·9 | ... | 8·3 |
| Printing and publishing | ... | ... | 7·1 | ... | ... |
| *Heavy industry* | 1·5 | 13 | 85 | 11·4 | 9·8 |
| Paper and paper products | 0·1 | 0·7 | 5·6 | 10·2 | 10·6 |
| Chemicals and chemical petroleum and coal products | 0·6 | 3·6 | 16·4 | 9·4 | 7·9 |
| Non-metallic mineral products | 0·3 | 1·2 | 5·2 | 7·2 | 7·6 |
| Basic metals | ... | 2·4 | 9·0 | 13·2 | 6·8 |
| Metal products | 0·7 | 5·6 | 49·6 | 12·9 | 11·2 |

*Source:* A. F. Ewing and S. J. Patel, op. cit., Table III.

\* Overall estimate of net industrial output distributed among the various sub-sectors on the basis of the structural pattern for class 4 in 1960, class 3 in 1980, and class 1 in 2000.

F

been disappointing. But they are a necessary part of the overall strategy of structural transformation. It is no paradox that without an increasing share of industry, structural transformation is impossible, but that serious industrialization is unrealistic without high agricultural growth rates.

The next step is to attempt to arrive at overall indications of net industrial output in Africa in 1980 and 2000. This is again a framework and draws on the experience of other countries which have passed through similar stages of development, on the basis of a UN study[3] which divides countries from the point of view of industrialization into four classes. The framework suggested here means that Africa would approximate to class 3 by 1980 and class 1 by the end of the century. The structure of industrial output for these two classes has been taken and applied to the total estimates of the net value of industrial output in Africa in 1980 and 2000. The results are shown in Table 4.

Total industrial output is assumed to increase at about 8 per cent in the first twenty years and 9 per cent in the second twenty years, with the growth rate of mining lower and that of manufacturing higher than the average. Within manufacturing, light industry expands appreciably more slowly than heavy industry. This is in line with both the arguments set out in Chapter I and the experience of other countries.

The final task is to translate this framework into targets or estimates of possibilities, by industrial sectors. As explained at the beginning of this chapter, it would be both impossible and out of place to enter into great detail. An illustrative approach has been adopted, based largely on intermediate goods, capital goods, and agro-based consumer goods, with the emphasis throughout on industries in all three sectors requiring, to be viable and successful, the markets of two or more African countries. It is true, of course, that there is a considerable range of industry feasible at the national level, even in a small country, and this indeed, as has been shown in Chapter II, has so far been the main strategy adopted in most African countries, particularly with respect to consumer goods. The limitations of this approach have been pointed out and the strategy adopted here is a deliberate one, on grounds of both principle and experience.[4]

Before turning to the specific industrial sectors which are examined here, a word should be said about construction. This sector accounts for a large share of GDP in African economies and figures largely in development plans. Except for a limited number of largely expatriate contractors, who of course account for a considerable share of total construction output, the industry is heterogeneous, small-scale, and labour-intensive. Apart, therefore, from its obviously essential character in every economy, however small, it has the advantage of being a large-scale employer of relatively unskilled labour. In the immediate future, apart from training programmes, a major problem is to ensure a vast increase in the domestic production of building materials, a problem examined below.[5]

The remainder of this chapter is concerned to set out within a comparatively short compass yet in quantitative terms the essence of what could be achieved in the way of industrial development in Africa in the next ten to fifteen years. The discussion is organized by the sector classification used in this study and, for the most part, the ECA sub-regional groupings. At the end the possibilities are summed up in a chart relating to 1980. This necessarily detailed consideration of a wide range of industry may be easier to follow if constant reference is made to this chart (facing p. 92).

The methodology of estimating is explained fully in the documents cited which have been prepared mainly by ECA; sometimes references to particular methods of estimating are made here. Broadly speaking, for consumer goods income elasticities of demand are used. For some intermediate and capital goods there are established methods specific to each commodity, based partly on historical experience in other countries and partly on technical coefficients, e.g. steel, cement, fertilizers, insecticides, motor-vehicle tyres. Some of the estimates are derived from established relationships between consumption of a given product and GDP. There is necessarily a much greater margin of error in all these estimates than similar ones for developed countries where there are not only better statistics but also established past trends over a period of years.

The locations suggested are based mainly on lowest delivered cost to centres of consumption (though a caution must be entered here about transport for reasons discussed in Chapter VII), with some allowance for sharing of industries equitably even at somewhat higher cost. The resource factor has normally a greater pull in Africa at this stage than the market factor. Here again the justification of each location proposed can be found in the documents cited.

Finally it must be added that the ECA recommendations are derived for the most part from what are called preliminary or 'pre-feasibility' studies. To move to the stage of the bankable project the recommendations for the factories and their locations have to be confirmed by detailed feasibility and often also engineering studies.

METALS

Three metals will be considered: iron and steel, aluminium, and copper; and in each the production both of the primary metal and of finished products, such as finished iron and steel, sections, wire, sheet; simple products fabricated in aluminium: sectors, sheet, and domestic utensils; and extruded and rolled copper manufactures.

Consumption of iron and steel products, primarily rails, bar, rod, sections, plate and sheet and tubes, is projected to rise at an annual rate of between 9 and 10 per cent.[6] This means that total consumption in 1970 and 1980 would be as follows (in thousand tons):

| *North Africa* | | *West Africa* | | *Central Africa* | | *East Africa* | | *Total* |
| *1970* | *1980* | *1970* | *1980* | *1970* | *1980* | *1970* | *1980* | |
| 2,000 | 4,520 | 930 | 2,150 | 340 | 830 | 680[a] | 1,530 | 9,030[b] |

(*a*) Excluding rails.
(*b*) Of the four sub-regions, i.e. excluding South Africa.

This is not a high rate of growth of steel consumption in countries at an early stage of development,[7] but is a more than sufficient basis for the establishment of iron and steel industries in each of the four sub-regions. Economies of scale are important in iron and steel making, and thinking is therefore based on sub-regionally co-ordinated projects, with phasing of development over a long period of time. Definite agreements have yet to be made, but the probable pattern is emerging.

In North Africa work is in progress at Annaba in Algeria on a plant which will have a crude steel capacity of 380,000 tons, based on domestic ore, to produce 300,000 tons of flat products. It is expected to come into production in 1967. In Tunisia a small integrated works based on domestic ore with an initial capacity of 80,000 tons and with provision for doubling it at a later stage, has now started production in the Menzel–Bourguiba region, to produce reinforcing bars and light sections. Both these works should be in operation by 1968. The Annaba works should be reasonably economic, but the Tunisian one will be high cost. In Morocco a re-rolling works is envisaged at Casablanca, with a capacity of 120,000 tons, possibly fed initially by billets from Annaba, as well as scrap. Later, an integrated plant with a capacity of 300,000 tons, based on domestic ore, is contemplated. The need for co-ordination of production in the Maghreb, particularly of rolling programmes, is apparent and negotiations are in progress. Before 1980 the market would justify further expansion.

The UAR is already an established producer, based on domestic ore. At present costs are high. There is a small integrated works at Helwan, producing flats and light and medium sections, and three semi-integrated plants producing together 180,000 tons of round bars. It is planned to expand Helwan to 1·5 million tons and to add there a 700,000-ton strip-mill. A second integrated plant is envisaged at Aswan, with a capacity of 400,000 tons of round bars. A wide plate mill with a capacity of 200,000 tons is under study and the semi-integrated plants are expected to double their capacity.

In East Africa, apart from scrap melting in Uganda and Ethiopia, there is only one producer, the Que-Que works in Rhodesia, with a pig-iron capacity of 250,000 tons, a crude steel capacity of 150,000 tons, and a wide range of finished products. There are expansion plans, modest in steel but extensive in pig iron (to over 800,000 tons), largely for export overseas, to take advantage of the high-grade iron ore and also good coking coal, which is rare in Africa.

A plan for co-ordinated development of iron and steel making in East Africa was presented to a conference on economic co-ordination held in Lusaka in 1965.[8] The proposals were for three integrated works each of about 500,000 tons capacity, at Que-Que (Rhodesia), Tororo (Uganda), and Lusaka or vicinity (Zambia), together with a large re-rolling works (250,000 tons) at Dar-es-Salaam (Tanzania) and 50,000-ton re-rolling works in Addis Ababa (Ethiopia) and in Madagascar, supplied with billets from the integrated works. The programme is phased in time, with the 1980 estimated market in view.

Co-ordinated proposals for Central Africa have also been drawn up,[9] although details remain to be elaborated and, as elsewhere, decisions to be taken. The Democratic Republic of the Congo has decided to set up an iron and steel works by electric reduction of ore in the Kinshasa area and based on Inga power, with a capacity of about 300,000 tons. A study is in progress as to the source of ore. This could be the first step in a Central African programme, phased over time, with the 1980 market in view. The next step might be a 400,000-ton integrated works at Owendo (Gabon) based on the extensive and high-grade Mekambo ore which can be expected to flow in the early seventies with the building of a railway to the coast. This works might be much larger if export outside Africa of cheap semi-finished steel proves feasible. However, consideration might also be given to a works at Pointe-Noire, based on the rich ore deposits in the Republic of the Congo. Both works are prima facie feasible in the long run.

There remains West Africa. Here again, co-ordinated proposals have been drawn up[10] and were presented to a conference on Industrial Co-ordination in West Africa held in Bamako in 1964. They involve a coastal works of 700,000 tons in Liberia (which, as in the case of Owendo, and for the same reasons, might be much bigger), and an inland works with a capacity of 200,000 tons in Mali. In arriving at the recommendation for the coastal works, four countries were examined on a detailed comparative basis: Liberia, Ghana, Nigeria, and Gabon (and the comparison was subsequently extended to Mauritania; it was also intended to consider Guinea, but it proved impossible to obtain data). A comparable basis was employed for the inquiry in terms of capacity and process—conventional blast furnace with imported coke and limestone, LD steel, continuous casting, and conventional rolling. In the case of Ghana and Nigeria, it was assumed that ore would be imported from Liberia or elsewhere in West Africa. The results expressed as a percentage of Lower-Buchanan (Liberia) in terms of total delivered costs (averaged out over the area of assumed distribution) were:

| | |
|---|---|
| Owendo | 109 |
| Port Harcourt | 120 |
| Tema | 117 |
| Port-Étienne | 127 |

The ex-works costs at Lower-Buchanan, expressed in terms of reinforcing rods, were estimated at US $88.00 per ton, a highly competitive figure on a world market basis.[11]

The ex-works costs estimated for the works proposed in Mali were much higher, but the basis of the whole scheme was the serving of internal markets, where transport costs of imported steel are high.

The Bamako conference accepted in principle works in Liberia and Mali, subject to noting that Nigeria intended to build a works to serve its own market, using its own comparatively low-grade ore and its coal (which is not coke-fiable). In fact, two years later Nigerian intentions are still unclear and its problems have been complicated by the conflicting pulls of its internal regions. All the proposals which have emerged so far are high cost in character.

Since Bamako, a committee of interested countries, serviced by Liberia and envisaged as an embryo West African Iron and Steel Authority, has been set up. But little progress has been made, since there remain too many candidates in the field, and the necessary firm agreements to purchase the output of the Liberian works are not yet forthcoming. This in turn has hampered the Liberian search for finance, despite the obvious attractiveness of their proposed works.

A solution should not be impossible, given a programme phased over a period of years. Liberia could supply much of the market of the coastal countries in the relevant range of finished steel products and also semis to re-rollers (one works already installed in Ghana), while Nigeria could start with re-rolling on a substantial scale, perhaps 250,000 tons, also using Liberian semis. Eventually a fully integrated works to supply Nigeria's own market would be amply justified. Mali will not be in a position to make iron and steel until the Gouina barrage is installed in the early seventies. A works there will find a natural outlet in the Senegal River Basin countries.

If all the schemes envisaged and outlined here are realized, there will be rather more than 7 million tons of capacity in operation (measured in crude steel equivalents) in Africa (excluding South Africa) by 1980, against a conservatively estimated demand of over 9 million. Since the whole range of finished products required could not be produced, this is a reasonable, perhaps conservative, programme and, with one or two exceptions, all the projects pay due regard to economies of scale. The temptation evidently remains to envisage still more projects. If this is not resisted, production will not be forthcoming, since investors, domestic or foreign, will not put money into a proliferation of small-scale, high-cost works.

Agreed decisions are now urgent. Some space has been devoted to iron and steel, since this industry is significant, in the double sense of its fundamental economic importance and because it is sought by most developing countries, for reasons which are in the last analysis sound. If the co-ordinated and rational programme now emerging is agreed and realized, the pace of development of the iron and steel industry will accelerate in the last two decades of this century and by the year 2000 production will be spread throughout many countries of the continent. It is the first step which is the difficult one, and if there is still some hard bargaining ahead in the next year or two, the shape of the programme now emerging is encouraging.

Africa has possibilities as a producer of aluminium. One reason is the presence of bauxite resources. The other, much more important, is cheap electric power. An illustration of this factor is that in Canada and Norway, cheap hydro-power producers, electric energy accounts for 7 per cent of ingot value, compared with about 20 per cent elsewhere.[12]

In the late fifties, these factors accounted for much interest in the locating in Africa of a substantial proportion of growing world production, notably in Ghana, Guinea, the Cameroon, and the two Congos. The Cameroon has, in fact, become the first African producer of aluminium metal and Ghana will be the second.

Guinea has not so far progressed beyond the alumina stage, although the principal African producer of bauxite. The Democratic Republic of the Congo is now thinking along different lines,[13] with agriculture and industrial development geared largely to the domestic market. On the other hand, the Republic of the Congo still has ambitions to become a major aluminium producer.[13] Throughout, excepting Guinea, where ample bauxite is also a factor, cheap hydro-power potential has been the main determinant.

In fact, it is now clear that the presence of bauxite is not a major element. There remains the electric power factor. In this respect, since the Democratic Republic of the Congo is adopting another approach, the Republic of the Congo would seem to be potentially better placed than other African countries, given that the power costs there would be lower than in Ghana and Guinea. In terms of hydro-power costs, Africa is as well or better placed than any other continent. At the same time, it is now generally considered that the time is near when nuclear energy, at a scale of 500 MW, will be as cheap as any other form thereof. Given the limited significance of bauxite in total costs, this may mean that Africa will no longer be a favoured location for production of aluminium metal for the world market.[14] Yet it should be borne in mind that from 1900 to 1960 world aluminium production doubled every seven years, a trend which is likely to continue for some time to come.

There remains the possibility of producing aluminium metal for African domestic markets. In 1963 consumption was 51,000 tons of which one-third was in South Africa. Current projections for 1980 lie between 75,000 and 114,000 tons. But it is argued that there are opportunities for much higher levels of consumption.[15] Such opportunities are in domestic utensils, canning, roofing (especially in agricultural buildings), piping (particularly for irrigation), house-building, electric power, and transportation. There are already between forty and fifty aluminium fabricating plants in Africa, producing mainly sheets and domestic utensils. Production is economic on a small scale and rapid expansion is feasible.

The only African country so far to lay down facilities for the production of aluminium is the Cameroon, which is also constructing rolling facilities. Tanzania also rolls aluminium and there is scope for others, provided always there is sub-regional co-operation. European and North American experience shows that aluminium has already made substantial inroads into the markets for other materials. This is likely to be even more true of Africa.

At present, copper metal is produced on a large scale in only two African countries, Zambia and the Democratic Republic of the Congo, almost entirely for export overseas. The world demand for copper is likely to continue to expand steadily and Africa may be in a position to increase its share of a growing world market, not only through the two existing major producers but also through new sources of production in the years to come, e.g. the Central African Republic and Mauritania. Copper is rolled and cables made in Rhodesia and Kenya.

African producers, though not the dominant financial interests concerned, have shown, for obvious reasons, an interest in proceeding from production of metal to first-stage processing, extrusion and rolling. The market for such products within Africa is likely to remain limited for some years to come. Export of copper manufactures would seem to be in itself an economic proposition, and the Far East in particular might prove to be a promising market.[16] But the highly cartelized arrangements in the world copper market are a serious obstacle. The start of a breakthrough must be within Africa, despite the limitations of the market. It has been suggested that, with the East African market in mind, Zambia should go in for brass alloying, a non-ferrous foundry, and possibly extrusion facilities to make wire rod.[17] Both the surveys cited seem to agree that the market is not yet sufficient to envisage the establishment of rolling facilities. However, their perspectives were for East Africa only, based on Zambia. A joint Zambian–Democratic Republic of the Congo programme with the whole African market in view would be likely to give rise to much wider possibilities and it is understood that discussions with this in view have been started.

### TIMBER PRODUCTS

Although Africa is an enormous timber producer and exporter and has substantial forest resources, it is in deficit, even in terms of existing low levels of consumption. The following figures illustrate the situation (in million units) :[18]

|  | Production | Imports | Exports | Consumption |
|---|---|---|---|---|
| Sawn wood (m³) | 2·88 | 1·85 | 0·73 | 4·00 |
| Plywood and veneer (m³) | 0·20 | 0·12 | 0·14 | 0·18 |
| Fibre board and particle board (tons) | 0·10 | 0·05 | 0·03 | 0·12 |
| Paper and paper board (tons) | 0·31 | 0·58 | 0·06 | 0·83 |
| Total in terms of wood raw materials (m³) | 7·44 | 5·87 | 2·07 | 11·24 |

There are differences from one sub-region to another. West Africa (which includes also Central Africa in the usage of the study cited) is in general a net exporter, which is hardly surprising. All the other sub-regions are in deficit, and especially North Africa.

The long-run perspectives for Africa as an exporter overseas of sawn wood, plywood and veneers, perhaps pulp and paper and certain other timber manufactures, are favourable;[19] a co-ordinated policy to take advantage of them, covering at least West and Central Africa, is obviously to be recommended. The possibilities in Kenya for major timber industries, including pulp and paper, should also be remembered. But in the present context the main issue is how far present import deficits can be eliminated and the growing consumption in Africa of timber and timber products can be met from domestic resources.

Many African countries could do more to exploit their timber resources and develop timber manufactures for their own markets. The economies of scale factor varies from one product to another. In saw-milling it is not particularly important, the main elements being raw material supplies available and the markets to be served, given the high incidence of transport costs. The scale factor is important in pulp and paper. Suitable and cheap raw materials are essential, but capital costs are high, and also power costs. Fixed investment costs, in US $1,000 per daily ton, have been estimated as follows (in ascending order of mill size):[20]

*Non-integrated*

| | | | | |
|---|---|---|---|---|
| Unbleached chemical pulp | 233 | 175 | 135 | 105 |
| Bleached chemical pulp | 325 | 240 | 190 | 150 |

*Integrated*

| | | | | |
|---|---|---|---|---|
| Unbleached paper | 300 | 230 | 180 | 140 |
| Bleached paper | 390 | 295 | 235 | 185 |

The scale factor is also important in plywood, veneers, fibre board, and particle board, though less so than in pulp and paper. There remain a wide range of forest products, feasible on a small scale, even though in the African context some degree of specialization would be advantageous. Such industries include builders' joinery, furniture, and packing cases. What is required essentially is more research, in both forestry proper and forest industries, including market research, together with training at the industrial level.[21]

A co-ordinated approach likely to be more practicable on a sub-regional basis is required, especially in research and training. But there is also clearly scope for co-operation in production policy and overseas marketing (particularly, so far as the last point is concerned, among the major timber-producing countries of West and Central Africa).

It has been estimated that to meet the African regions' domestic requirements (requirements in investment for export are excluded) of forest products by 1975, the following increases in capacity and consequential investment are necessary:[22]

|  |  | *Million US dollars* |
|---|---|---|
| Sawn wood | 2 to 3 million m$^3$ | 60 |
| Wood-based panels | 600,000 m$^3$ | 70 to 170 |
| Pulp and paper | 1·5 million tons | 800 |

It is evident that a co-ordinated production programme is vital wherever economies of scale are important, and especially in pulp and paper, not least (as in the case of iron and steel) to attract the necessary finance.

### BASIC BUILDING MATERIALS

In addition to iron and steel, aluminium, and timber (and plastics, to be considered later), the basic building materials are bricks and other clay products, cement and derivatives, particularly concrete and asbestos-cement, and glass. Bricks and other clay products are not considered here. They are normally small-scale local industries since the raw material is widespread, economies of scale are not of much importance, and transport costs are high.

Cement is a key product, the output of which depends primarily on the occurrence of suitable grades of limestone, although countries without this can make cement by importing and grinding clinker. The economies of scale are significant but are quickly offset by the high costs of transport, so that acceptable delivered costs can be achieved in an inland country at an output as low as 40,000 to 50,000 tons. When a scale of output of 100,000 tons and upwards is possible, distinct savings can be obtained compared with the delivered cost of imported cement. It follows that even today most African countries with limestone deposits can produce cement economically and indeed much progress has been made. Only about 25 per cent of cement consumed in Africa is imported, mainly in West and Central Africa. On the other hand, there is no room for complacency, since demand rises fast, 6 per cent per annum from 1953 to 1963,[23] and is likely to rise even faster in the future.

Scope for multi-national development lies for all practical purposes (and leaving aside special grades of cement) in Central and parts of West Africa. In Central Africa the Republic of the Congo is building a works with a capacity of 100,000 tons, designed also to supply clinker to the Central African Republic. A works is being planned in northern Cameroon, to supply also Chad, with an initial capacity of 30,000 to 45,000 tons. A works is being planned in Gabon, to supply also southern Cameroon with clinker, with a capacity of over 100,000 tons. It might be preferable to postpone the northern works and expand cement capacity in Gabon and clinker-grinding capacity in southern Cameroon. In West Africa there is a project to produce 200,000 tons in Dahomey, partly to supply clinker to Ghana, Nigeria, and the Ivory Coast. Upper Volta could produce cement, both for its own market and for northern Ghana and the Ivory Coast. Other countries which are likely to have to rely on imported clinker (or cement) are Liberia, Mauritania, and Sierra Leone.

Concrete products can be produced on a small scale. On the other hand, economies of scale are quite significant for asbestos-cement, with 5,000 tons as a minimum size and clear advantages at 15,000 to 25,000 tons. Sub-regional co-operation is therefore required and it is estimated that there would be scope for perhaps a dozen plants in Africa by 1970.[24]

Glass is another industry where economies of scale are important. This is not so significant for glass bottles, although the variety of end products makes co-ordination an advantage. But in the case of flat glass, 6,000 tons at the minimum and 10,000 tons or more is desirable. On this basis, some eight plants are estimated as necessary by 1970.[24]

Comprehensive estimates have been made of the demand for building materials in Africa, together with a detailed examination of production possibilities and prospects.[25] The benefits to be derived from a bold expansion programme have been calculated in terms of a ten-year period, covering cement, clay products, asbestos-cement, flat glass, iron and steel, and timber products, and, compared with what would have to be imported in the absence of such a programme, an investment cost of about US $2,000 million would be required, which would represent not more than one-eighth of expenditure on building materials, cumulated over the period, and two-fifths of the savings in foreign currency which would be obtained if locally produced materials were substituted for imports.[26]

## THE CHEMICAL INDUSTRY

The main starting-point for a chemical industry in Africa is logically fertilizer manufacture. This partly because of the need to provide inputs to agriculture and partly because production of fertilizers requires production of basic chemicals which leads on to production of other chemicals. In this brief consideration of Africa's possibilities, the first step therefore is prospects for fertilizers. This, is followed by pesticides, key acids and alkalis, petro-chemicals, and, finally, miscellaneous products which are in demand and capable of being produced, such as viscose rayon, calcium carbide, and aluminium sulphate.[27] Industries such as paints, varnishes, perfumes, and pharmaceuticals are not examined here, mainly because at this stage of development the value added is limited (although the scope for moving backwards is considerable). Small national industries such as industrial gases are also not considered. The approach is towards a basic chemical industry as a major factor in economic development. And since this is a capital-intensive industry, where economies of scale are decisive, a co-ordinated sub-regional and even a regional approach is essential.

There are three major fertilizers: nitrogen, phosphate, and potash. These are delivered to the farmer in varying combinations, depending on local conditions. In developed countries, what are known as mixed fertilizers are becoming increasingly popular, and the same trend can be expected in Africa. Fertilizer mixing is possible on a relatively small scale.

The first step is to get an idea of the potential demand for fertilizers. This is a difficult exercise, since it involves an examination in some detail of the specific agricultural characteristics (soils, crops, climate, method of farming, etc.) and potential of many different countries. Global methods, which are useful enough for steel and cement, for example, are of little value. Forecasts have been made by the ECA/FAO, using a variety of methods,[28] as follows (in terms of 1,000 tons of pure nutrient and including, in this instance, South Africa):

| *Nitrogen (N)* | | | *Phosphorus ($P_2O_5$)* | | | *Potassium ($K_2O$)* | | |
|---|---|---|---|---|---|---|---|---|
| *1961–62* | *1970* | *1980* | *1961–62* | *1970* | *1980* | *1961–62* | *1970* | *1980* |
| 366·0 | 957·0 | 2265·0 | 276·0 | 948·0 | 1960·0 | 104·0 | 353·0 | 985·0 |

These estimates are likely to be on the conservative side,[29] but are in themselves a sufficient basis for producing fertilizers in Africa.

The cost of production of nitrogen fertilizer depends primarily on the cost of ammonia. This can be manufactured in various ways, and in particular from natural gas, naphtha and other petroleum feedstocks, or electrolysis. It is now well established that the three processes mentioned are in ascending order of cost and that the first two only are of real interest from an economic point of view.[30] Economies of scale are such that the minimum level of output is of the order of 50,000 tons per annum. Production of 60,000 tons of ammonia and 225,000 tons of ammonium sulphate has been recommended in West Africa, in Nigeria, based on natural gas. This is to be followed by fertilizer plants of 60,000 tons ammonia capacity in Ghana and in Senegal.

In Central Africa the estimated future market by 1975 is about sufficient to justify a nitrogen plant, though present consumption estimates are probably conservative. Ammonium sulphate is again the appropriate fertilizer. There is suitable natural gas in the Cameroon, and an alternative possibility is naphtha from the refinery being erected in the Democratic Republic of the Congo. It should, of course, be one or the other.

Central Africa, in the present context, includes the western Congo. In the east, at Lake Kivu, there is also natural gas, a promising prospect, subject to more detailed technical study, for eastern Congo, Rwanda, Burundi, and western Uganda. A precise location for a nitrogen fertilizer plant has to be established, with Rwanda perhaps the strongest candidate. For the rest of East Africa, two plants have been proposed, one at Umtali (Rhodesia), to produce 100,000 tons of ammonia, 190,000 tons of ammonium sulphate, 80,000 tons of ammonium nitrate, and 14,000 tons of explosives; and the other at Mombasa (Kenya) with an output of 50,000 tons of ammonia and 190,000 tons of ammonium sulphate. In each case, ammonia would be produced from naphtha.

North Africa is much more advanced in both production and consumption of fertilizers. There is an advanced project to produce 350,000 tons of ammonia, 175,000 tons of ammonium nitrate, and 140,000 tons of urea from natural gas in Algeria. There is also a plan for 330,000 tons of ammonia in Libya, based on natural gas. These quantities considerably exceed Maghreb requirements, but at this scale of output export overseas can be envisaged. The UAR produces a wide range of fertilizers and the Sudan plans to produce ammonium nitrate from naphtha.

There are two natural locations for phosphate fertilizer in West Africa, Senegal and Togo, and plants with respective initial capacities of 45,000 tons of triple and 180,000 tons of single superphosphate have been recommended. The former is expected to expand to 85,000 tons and the latter to fall to 135,000 tons; but in Togo in addition to single superphosphate, production of 100,000 tons of triple superphosphate is envisaged, to be doubled later. Construction is under way in Senegal. A plant in Togo could also conveniently supply Central Africa, where phosphate deposits are low-grade and production unlikely for a long time to come. In East Africa there are already two plants producing superphosphates, in Rhodesia and Uganda, and its is expected that they will be enlarged. A third plant has been recommended to produce 160,000 tons of single superphosphate in Dar-es-Salaam (Tanzania). North Africa is, of course, a major producer and exporter of both phosphate rock and fertilizer.

Potash is not widely distributed in Africa. There are two major plants under construction, one in the Republic of the Congo and the other in Ethiopia, both planning to produce about 600,000 tons of potash (of 60 per cent $K_2O$) by 1970, and both, of course, based largely on world markets.

There is clearly scope for a significant move forward in the production of fertilizers, and indeed, as demand grows, it may be that present plans are somewhat conservative. There is also much to be said for deliberately stimulating demand[31] and this in turn is facilitated by domestically available supply.

There is a wide range of pesticides on the market. The two most important in Africa are DDT and BHC. Demand for DDT in East and West Africa in 1970 is estimated at, respectively, 5,250 and 2,900 tons of 75 per cent. The corresponding figures for BHC are 3,480 and 10,000 tons of 25 per cent. Capacity could be installed to match the estimated demand. The locations proposed in West Africa, the determining factors being cheap salt and cheap electric power, are probably Ghana, Guinea, and Senegal: salt electrolysis at Souapiti (Guinea), with manufacture of DDT in Ghana, Guinea, and Senegal, and BHC in Guinea. In East Africa, Umtali (Rhodesia) and Nairobi (Kenya) have been recommended. In

Central Africa a caustic soda/chlorine complex is being examined in the Democratic Republic of the Congo, based on Inga power.

Pesticides have been considered at this stage in line with the strategy followed in this study, that the starting-point of an African chemical industry is inputs for agriculture. However, from a production point of view, caustic soda, chlorine, BHC, DDT, and PVC are combined, and it is caustic soda which, in terms of consumption, is the primary determining factor. This is widely used in industry in soap-making, textiles, vegetable oil treatment, the treatment of bauxite, pulp and paper, rayon, and petroleum refining. The locations proposed in West Africa are Nigeria, Ghana, Guinea, and Senegal, with capacities of approximately 15,000, 7,000, 18,000, and 7,000 tons respectively in 1970, excepting the last figure, which is for 1980. DDT and BHC have already been discussed. PVC (20,000 tons) has been recommended for Nigeria for 1971. In East Africa, production of 13,500 tons of caustic soda has been recommended in Nairobi and 7,500 tons in Umtali. Production of 7,000 tons of PVC has also been proposed in Nairobi. In Central Africa, the whole caustic/chlorine complex seems likely to be in the Democratic Republic of the Congo, on the coast near Matadi and close to the Inga site.

Although caustic soda produced by salt electrolysis is now the cheapest method of production, there is the problem, serious in developing countries, of finding adequate outlets for chlorine. This is an additional reason, therefore, for stimulating demand for pesticides and PVC. Mention should also be made of soda ash. Kenya is a major producer, and Lake Chad may be another potential source.

The principal acid is sulphuric, the major user being the fertilizer industry and especially superphosphates. Present capacity (excluding South Africa) is of the order of rather less than 1 million tons, 60 per cent in North Africa. Expansion plans in hand will raise capacity to nearly 2 million tons, mainly in North Africa. It would seem necessary to envisage a total African capacity of over 3 million tons by 1970. Economies of scale are not of major importance and capacity should be able to expand in accordance with requirements. The main difficulty is that most of the sulphur has to be imported. This has given rise to a search for substitute acids, and especially hydrochloric, which is another outlet for chlorine. Research is also proceeding on the substitution of nitric acid, of

G

particular interest to countries with petroleum or natural gas resources.

The main products derived from petro-chemicals are ammonia and nitrogen fertilizers (already considered), plastics, synthetic fibres, synthetic rubber, and a miscellaneous group already partly examined, including benzine, detergents, insecticides, solvents, acetone, and carbon black. This is one of the major growth industries of the post-war period and plastics especially have to be considered carefully. Production of plastic manufactures, feasible on a small scale, is increasing rapidly, but on the basis of imported raw material. Petro-chemical technology is complex and large amounts of capital are required. None the less, given Africa's resources and the importance of the growing range of end-products, an immediate start on this industry would seem essential.

Algeria is at present the most favourable location. Plans are taking shape and may be referred to briefly. Based on natural gas at Arzew, not only ammonia but also methanol, acetylene, and PVC are envisaged. Based on the cracking of naphtha from the refinery at Algiers, products such as $C_4$-cut, polypropylene, or polyethylene are envisaged. Export markets are also aimed at, and the United Nations Special Fund is assisting in the carrying out of a major inquiry. The UAR is at present further advanced than Algeria, but its aim is mainly at domestic markets. The current plan envisages, among other products, polyethylene, PVC, phenol, acrytonitrile, caprolactam, polybutadiene, and methyl alcohol. Libya has possibilities comparable to those of Algeria, but plans are not yet very far advanced.

South of the Sahara, the petro-chemical industry is still at the stage of preliminary examination. Nigeria's natural gas resources are an obvious point of departure. Apart from ammonia and PVC, already referred to, consideration is being given to polyethylene and carbon black. The oil refineries in Senegal, the Ivory Coast, and Ghana, and that planned in Guinea might be other points of departure for ethylene, acetylene, benzine, and perhaps eventually synthetic fibres. The natural gas resources in Central Africa, Cameroon, and Gabon, still not fully explored, also come into the picture. High-pressure polyethylene is recommended for production in Dar-es-Salaam for the East African market. An agreement probably on a regional scale would seem essential in this field.

There remain some miscellaneous products which are candidates for early production in Africa. Industrial explosives are consumed in Africa mainly by the mining industry. Production is normally integrated with an ammonium nitrate plant; Nigeria and Rhodesia are the natural locations, and perhaps also a plant based on Lake Kivu natural gas.

Demand for viscose rayon is at a level and is increasing fast enough to justify manufacture in West and East Africa (and, of course, North Africa). In East Africa a plant with a capacity of 20,000 tons is recommended at Livingstone (Zambia) and another of 24,000 tons in Ethiopia. In West Africa one with a capacity of 16,000 tons is proposed for Nigeria and another with the same capacity for Ivory Coast. Apart from pulp, viscose rayon manufacture depends on sulphuric acid and caustic soda, and also carbon disulphide, suggested for production in Nigeria (7,000 tons). Within the framework of viscose rayon production in Livingstone, manufacture of sodium xanthate (manufactured from carbon disulphide and used as a flotation agent in the treatment of non-ferrous ores) is recommended (3,650 tons). It is evident that the backward linkage effects of viscose rayon are considerable.

Calcium carbide is an intermediate product for the manufacture of acetylene. A plant is being laid down in the UAR and production has been envisaged in Mali, based on the Gouina barrage, and in Dahomey, based on the Mono River barrage. Aluminium sulphate is used in paper sizing and water purification. Production is already taking place in Rhodesia and is planned in the UAR. Economies of scale are not significant and there would seem to be scope for at least one plant in each sub-region. Production can readily be incorporated with a sulphuric acid unit in a country which is a source of bauxite. Sodium silicate is used in the glass industry for sizing and in adhesives and detergents. Economies of scale are low and demand is increasing, so that there is scope for several plants.

## METAL MANUFACTURES

This industrial sector includes four distinct branches: metal products, mechanical engineering, electrical engineering, and transport equipment, each in turn comprising many industrial products. It has been shown in Chapter II that while there is a fair range of production of simple metal goods, the other branches are relatively blank, both in terms of what exists and what is planned, and that here lies the heart of Africa's industrial problem, the lack of capital goods industries. For this reason, and also because the information available is much less abundant than in the case of other industries considered in this chapter, discussion is necessarily in rather general or illustrative terms.[32]

Estimates of future demand for metal manufactures are difficult to make and a satisfactory methodology has not yet been worked out. There have been rough attempts for East and for Central Africa, using as a base-line past imports, the data thereon having been prepared largely by the Economic Commission for Europe from detailed world trade statistics in engineering products. It seems doubtful whether it is worth reproducing these estimates here; they underlie the proposals summarized below for new production.

The line between the making of metals and conversion is not a completely clear one. This is evident, for example, from the wide range of finished steel products classified within the steel industry and the similar techniques used in manufacture in the final stage of steel finishing and in the manufacture of a number of metal products. Wire drawing and the making of wire products, nails, screws, fasteners, plain wire, barbed wire and fencing, wire rope, and cables are at the dividing line. The scale of output can be quite low. These products are widely demanded in a developing economy, many of them in the agricultural sector. Wire drawing itself should be sub-regionally co-ordinated, but for several other products most African countries could be producers, although there is some scope for specialization owing to the wide range of specifications.

Tubes and pipes are sometimes classified with the steel industry and the range of final products is almost infinite. Requirements in a developing economy grow rapidly, for transport of oil and gas, in irrigation, in construction, in farm machinery, and for the manufacture of bicycles. For a considerable time to come, only certain types of tube and pipe (some kinds of welded tube and centrifugally cast pipes, for example) are feasible, and then only on the basis of sub-regional specialization, except that welded tubes are feasible on a small scale.

The casting of iron and steel in foundries is also basic to development and feasible on a small scale. The main outlets are standard parts for such consumer goods as stoves, hydraulic casting for pipes and fittings, and the casting of steel for wheels, axles, and buffers.

Boiler-making is another industry feasible in Africa, given some degree of specialization. It includes not only boilers as such but also steam generators, installations for refineries, tanks, and containers and bottles, formed sheets and plates, and welding. The common factors are bending, forming, and welding.

These basic activities in the first-stage transformation of metals have been set out systematically because they are the first and essential step. There are other simple metal products less easy to classify: steelwork such as bridges, pylons, structural elements for industrial, agricultural, commercial, and domestic building; and miscellaneous products made by stamping, forging, and welding, leading to, for example, metal windows, metal furniture, domestic appliances and utensils, hand tools, and metal packing materials.

It will be seen that metal products include consumer, intermediate, and capital goods and it has also been shown that some progress has been made in many African countries. But there is much to be done, at the national level, and through co-operation among small groups of countries. In this area, unlike iron and steel and basic chemicals, large groups at a sub-regional or even wider level are not normally necessary.

The proposals for expansion of production available at present relate mainly to East and to Central Africa. For the other parts of Africa they have to be regarded as tentative or illustrative. Nevertheless, it is of interest to set out examples of multi-national projects. Thus in East Africa a works to make bridges and heavy structures with an output of 10,000 tons per annum (t/p.a.) has been proposed for Zambia. Four works for light structures are regarded as justified, in Uganda, Kenya, Tanzania, and Rhodesia. Two works are proposed to make tanks, vats, and compressed-gas cylinders, in Kenya and Rhodesia. One works is considered sufficient for drawing wire for ropes, cables, and tyre wires, with an output of 40,000 to 50,000 t/p.a.; and another for drawing wire for fencing netting and wire gauze, with an output of 30,000 t/p.a. Three wire rope and cable works, two wire gauze and netting works, one fencing grills works, six plants to make nails, screws, etc., five works to produce hand tools, five to make hollow-ware and enamel ware, and two to make domestic stoves, are proposed, with the distribution balanced throughout the sub-region. In

Central Africa one plant is proposed for heavy structures, in the Republic of the Congo, two for light structures, in the same country and in the Cameroon, three for nails, screws, etc., two for hand tools, two for metal furniture, and two for metal frames and fixtures.

The next group to be considered is mechanical engineering, where there is at present much less capacity already installed. The techniques of production are generally more advanced and economies of scale usually more significant. The types of machinery required at the present stage of development in Africa are evident and it should suffice for present purposes to give illustrations of what has been proposed. In East Africa two plants are recommended to produce internal combustion engines in Kenya and in Zambia, each to produce 8,000 to 10,000 t/p.a. One tractor factory is suggested for Tanzania, to produce 14,000 to 16,000 units, and six plants to make agricultural machinery, especially ploughs. On the other hand, only one factory for harvesting, threshing, and sowing machines is regarded as justified, in Kenya, to produce 7,000 to 8,000 t/p.a. One plant is proposed for office machinery, in Kenya. In the machine-tool group, one plant is proposed for drilling, in Zambia, 2,000 t/p.a.; one for metal-cutting saws, in Tanzania, 1,000 t/p.a.; one for lathes, in Kenya, 3,000 t/p.a.; two for milling, in Kenya and Rhodesia, 4,000 to 5,000 t/p.a. each; and five for tool grinding, 200 t/p.a. each. Textile machinery production is suggested for Kenya, 8,000 to 10,000 t/p.a. Two plants are proposed for domestic sewing machines, in Kenya and Rhodesia, 50 to 60 t/p.a. each. Four plants are proposed for excavating machines, 5,000 to 6,000 t/p.a. each, and one for stone-crushing, in Uganda, 6,000 to 10,000 t/p.a. One plant is proposed for cocks, taps, and valve works, in Zambia, 3,000 to 5,000 t/p.a. Five plants for light, and four for medium-sized pumps, around 3,000 t/p.a. each, four for weighing machines, and four for winches and hoisting equipment, are all proposed.

In Central Africa the market is smaller. Agricultural machinery is proposed in each of the two Congos, 500 to 600 t/p.a. each. Simple machine tools are proposed in the Cameroon, 200 t/p.a., and the Democratic Republic of the Congo, 1,200 t/p.a. Sewing machines, 25,000 items, and office machines, 100,000 items, are also proposed for this last country. Scales are proposed for the Cameroon, 1,500 t/p.a.; saw blades for the Republic of the Congo,

500 t/p.a.; and lifting gear, both in this last country and in the Cameroon, 1,500 t/p.a. each.

North Africa is already more advanced, especially the UAR, where the range of mechanical engineering proposed above and more already exists, most of it installed in the last decade.

The data available on electrical engineering are inadequate. Small electrical cookers are feasible in most countries and the markets of two or three would suffice for assembly of domestic radio receivers, electric bulbs and lamps, transformers, and electric water heaters. In terms of East Africa the whole sub-regional market is considered essential to justify one factory each for electric motors, motor starters, electric fans, dry batteries, and domestic washing machines. In Central Africa domestic radio assembly is suggested in Gabon and the Republic of the Congo; transformers in the Cameroon and the Democratic Republic of the Congo; domestic refrigerators in the Cameroon and the Democratic Republic of the Congo; domestic heaters in the Cameroon; electric light bulbs in the same country; and dry batteries in Gabon. Several plants have been proposed for West Africa for batteries and accumulators, space heaters and domestic appliances, electric motors up to 10 kW, transformers up to 25 kVA, as well as switches and accessories.

Once again, North Africa is more advanced, especially the UAR which has now moved into production of electric power generating equipment.

There remains transport equipment. Here again the types likely to be demanded in Africa on an increasing scale are fairly evident. Illustrations on the proposals made for expansion of capacity are again set out, with existing repair facilities for railway equipment and motor vehicles as the starting-point.

First, East Africa. Two plants for the manufacture of railway freight cars are proposed in East Africa, one in Kenya and the other in Rhodesia, each 12,000 to 15,000 t/p.a. The manufacture of wheel sets is proposed in Rhodesia, 8,000 to 10,000 t/p.a. Production of railway cars is recommended in Tanzania, 60,000 to 70,000 units p.a. Five plants are suggested for assembly of buses, heavy commercial vehicles, and lorries, each 6,000 to 8,000 t/p.a. Six plants are proposed for the manufacture of motor-vehicle spare parts, each of 2,000 to 3,000 t/p.a. Eleven plants are proposed for the assembly and partial manufacture of bicycles.

In Central Africa commercial vehicle assembly is recommended in the Republic of the Congo and the Cameroon, 4,000 and 6,000 items respectively; bicycles in four of the six countries (including motor-bikes in the Cameroon); and railway rolling stock in the Republic of the Congo and the Cameroon, 1,500 t/p. a. each.

Assembly of motor vehicles is of limited interest owing to the low value added without progressive manufacture of components. The danger is that as in Latin America and to some extent North Africa, assembly will become a device for the motor-vehicle interests in the advanced countries to retain their markets, using assembly as a means of getting around high tariff barriers on complete vehicles, with disastrous consequences in proliferation of types and high costs. An example of what could be done in the Maghreb towards progressive manufacture of components within the framework of co-ordination and standardization is as follows:

A high degree of standardization and the co-ordination of types among the Maghreb countries would allow production of different parts on a sufficient scale to make costs competitive. Establishing a minimum scale of requirements on a standardization basis for engines, axles, gear boxes, etc., would facilitate assembly and also make possible production of, for example, pistons and valves. At a later stage, production of more advanced components would be possible, e.g. the machining of forged parts imported in a rough state and the manufacture of parts of the chassis. The range of products could be increased steadily so that up to 80 to 85 per cent of the work could be done in North Africa, taking into account also the contribution of the textile industry, plastic components, the chemical industry for glues, paints and varnishes, the glass industry (which could also produce safety glass), the forging that could be done, tyres and other rubber items and accessories such as batteries and cables.[33]

Another transport industry where assembly and progressive manufacture of components is possible is shipbuilding, mainly for coastal ships and river craft.

Metal manufactures are one of the principal keys to a serious approach to economic development, following logically on and stimulated by installation of facilities for the production of basic metals. Moreover, unlike these metals and chemicals, capital intensity is often quite low, with obvious advantages from the point of view of allocation of investment resources and the creation of new employment opportunities. This is also the industrial sector *par excellence* which generates new skills and a real industrial climate. One last point, particularly from the point of view of co-ordination among countries: standardization, to be considered later, is of vital importance.

### MAJOR AGRO-BASED CONSUMER GOODS

For reasons given earlier in this chapter, little space will be devoted here to consumer goods and most of those considered are agro-based. Many of them are relatively easy to establish. Within an overall policy of industrial co-ordination it would be sensible to leave such industries primarily to countries which have natural comparative advantage, particularly since such countries are often those which, at least in the next decade or so, have little potentiality for capital goods industries.

In the case of food industries there are several which are well established, capable of expansion, and geared primarily to overseas export markets, e.g. edible and other vegetable oils, and the canning of fruit, fruit juices, and vegetables. These industries need not be considered here. There are three other major food industries (leaving aside cereals, including rice, which depend primarily on agriculture): sugar, fish, and meat.

The economies of scale in sugar manufacture are important, together with natural conditions, and large-scale production is therefore confined to a relatively small number of countries, several in East Africa (including Madagascar), the Republic of the Congo (which expects to become a major exporter), and with production planned in the Cameroon and Chad. Production on an artisanal scale is possible, but specialization seems more sensible.

Fishing is another industry with major expansion prospects, including overseas markets; processing and preservation is a substantial operation. It goes without saying that the coastal countries have an advantage, but there are also distinct possibilities inland in countries such as Chad owing to the major rivers feeding Lake Chad.

Meat of some sort can be produced in almost all African countries, but there are some with genuine comparative advantage, particularly if breeding, feeding, and veterinary services can be improved. Such countries are to be found in the hinterland of West and Central Africa, including Mali, Upper Volta, Niger, northern Nigeria, Chad, and northern Cameroon; and Ethiopia and Kenya in East Africa. Development of a major meat industry is expensive, not only owing to the improvements to which attention has already been drawn but also the laying down of refrigeration, storage, and transport facilities. Logically, the countries mentioned should be encouraged to supply part of the requirements of the protein-hungry countries of the coast and also think in terms of large-scale exports to world markets.

Almost all countries are planning a textile industry, whether cotton growers or not. The presence of domestic cotton is not in itself a decisive locational factor. Spinning and weaving, at least, are possible at a relatively low scale of output. But it should be remembered that there is some advantage in having local cotton and some degree of economies of scale, so that, bearing in mind also the general need for industrial co-ordination, it would be sound policy to allow the inland countries to shoulder the largest part of the burden. Some of these countries can hope ultimately to become exporters of textiles in world markets, as is already true of the UAR. This in turn would enable scarce investment resources in countries elsewhere to be applied to other lines of industry, in which they have comparative advantage.

The main reasons why the UAR is able not only to supply the varied and growing domestic market but also to export competitively are, first, that it has one of the best-quality cottons in the world, and secondly, that it has deliberately pursued a policy of installing, with the help of producers in the United Kingdom and the United States, advanced finishing processes. These factors, coupled with relatively cheap and increasingly skilled labour and the installation of the most modern textile machinery obtained from the United Kingdom, the United States, Switzerland, and Germany, readily explain the UAR's strong position.

The scope for import substitution of textiles in Africa is of course formidable, as can be seen from the following figures (given in million square yards) :[34]

|  | East Africa | Central Africa | West Africa |
|---|---|---|---|
| Current output | 200 | 102 | 220 |
| Current demand | 870 | 262 | 1,050 |
| Target production, 1975 | 1,300 | 276 | 1,125 |

It will be seen that current demand will be barely exceeded by 1975 in Central and West Africa but substantially exceeded in East Africa. However, demand in 1975 will be much higher, so that all three regions seem likely to remain in substantial deficit. Comparable figures for North Africa are not available, but the aim is to wipe out import dependence, for all practical purposes, by the early seventies. In West Africa the main textile producer at present is Nigeria, but there are plans for expansion of existing or new production thereof in several countries. Those which, on the basis of the principles set out here, seem to be indicated as specialists are Mali, Niger, Upper Volta, the Ivory Coast, and Nigeria.

In Central Africa the appropriate locations are the cotton-growing countries: Chad, the Central African Republic, and northern Cameroon (with a substantial industry installed). A pattern of specialization along these lines may well emerge. In East Africa the specialists are Ethiopia, which is already approaching self-sufficiency, Kenya, Uganda, which would seem to be particularly well placed, and Tanzania. In North Africa, as already shown, the UAR has an advanced textile industry, and although less extensive, there is significant production in Morocco, Tunisia, and the Sudan.

From all this it follows that it would seem more reasonable for such countries as Senegal, Guinea, Liberia, Ghana, Gabon, the Republic of the Congo, Algeria, Libya, and Zambia not to think of textiles on any scale at this stage, in view of all the other industrial opportunities open to them. The same may be true of the Democratic Republic of the Congo, Kenya, and Rhodesia, so far as further expansion of this industry is concerned. The discussion so far has been based on cotton textiles. Different possibilities arise with synthetics, already considered in this chapter.

The prospects of increasing production of leather goods of all kinds are also evident. Here again, it would seem sensible to try, within the framework of industrial co-ordination, to concentrate production as far as possible on the cattle-producing countries. Similarly, specialization is indicated for rubber manufactures: tyres, footwear, industrial belting, etc. The appropriate countries are, for example, the Cameroon, the Democratic Republic of the Congo, Liberia, and Nigeria.

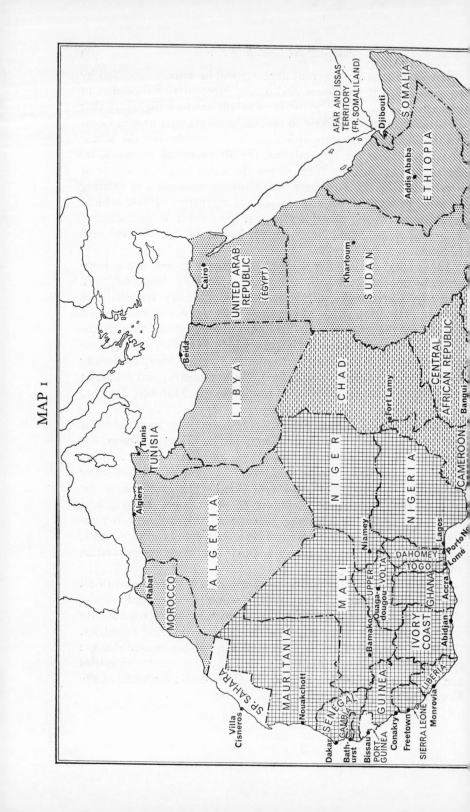

MAP 1

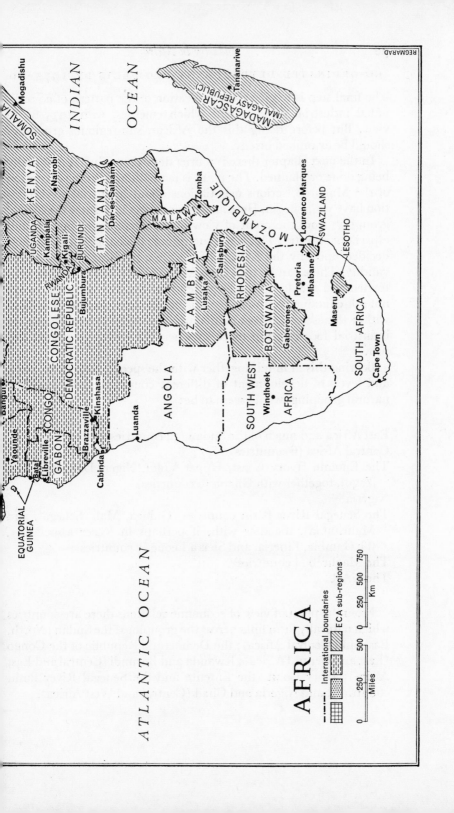

AFRICA

International boundaries
ECA sub-regions

Miles
0    250    500    750
0  250  500  750
Km

ATLANTIC OCEAN

EQUATORIAL
GUINEA

Yaounde

Bata

Libreville  CONGO

GABON

Brazzaville

Cabinda

Luanda

ANGOLA

SOUTH WEST
AFRICA

Windhoek

Bangui

CONGOLESE
DEMOCRATIC REPUBLIC

Kinshasa

RWANDA
Kigali
BURUNDI
Bujumbura

UGANDA
Kampala

Nairobi

KENYA

SOMALIA

Mogadishu

INDIAN

OCEAN

TANZANIA
Dar-es-Salaam

MALAWI
Zomba

ZAMBIA

Lusaka

Salisbury

RHODESIA

BOTSWANA

Gaberones

Pretoria
Mbabane

SWAZILAND

Lourenco Marques

LESOTHO

Maseru

SOUTH AFRICA

Cape Town

MADAGASCAR
(MALAGASY REPUBLIC)

Tananarive

REGMARAD

CO-ORDINATED DEVELOPMENT PROSPECTS BY 1975–80

The final step is to give some indication of the pattern of co-ordi-nated industrial development which emerges, with 1975–80 in view. But before doing this the African sub-regional groupings should be examined briefly.

In the next chapter there is a brief discussion of what is actually being done or planned. The point is made that, with the exception of the Maghreb, serious negotiations about industrial co-ordina-tion have yet to begin. Here an attempt is made to show the logical groupings from the point of view of economic development, and especially industry. This is not to presume to change the groupings decided upon by the ECA, which have a political and economic validity. These can be seen from Map 1. Yet it has never been in-tended and should not be forgotten that the four sub-regions are not self-contained entities; nor do they exclude smaller groupings within themselves. These points are of particular importance for industrial location, the more so when the transport system im-proves. [35]

Bearing this in mind, together with the specific structures, sizes, and levels of development of different countries, the immediate natural groupings would seem to be:

East Africa and much of the Sudan (12 countries)
Central Africa (6 countries)
The Entente (Ivory Coast, Upper Volta, Niger, Dahomey, and
    Togo), together with Ghana (6 countries)
Nigeria
The Senegal River Basin countries (Guinea, Mali, Senegal, and
    Mauritania), together with, if perhaps in looser association,
    the Gambia, Liberia, and Sierra Leone (7 countries)
The Maghreb (4 countries)
The UAR

From the point of view of economic relations there are countries which naturally form links across the groupings: the Sudan (North, East, and Central Africa); the Democratic Republic of the Congo (East and Central Africa); Rwanda and Burundi (Central and East Africa); Ivory Coast (the Entente and the Senegal River Basin countries); and Nigeria and Chad (Central and West Africa).

An outline of possible industrial development in Africa by 1980

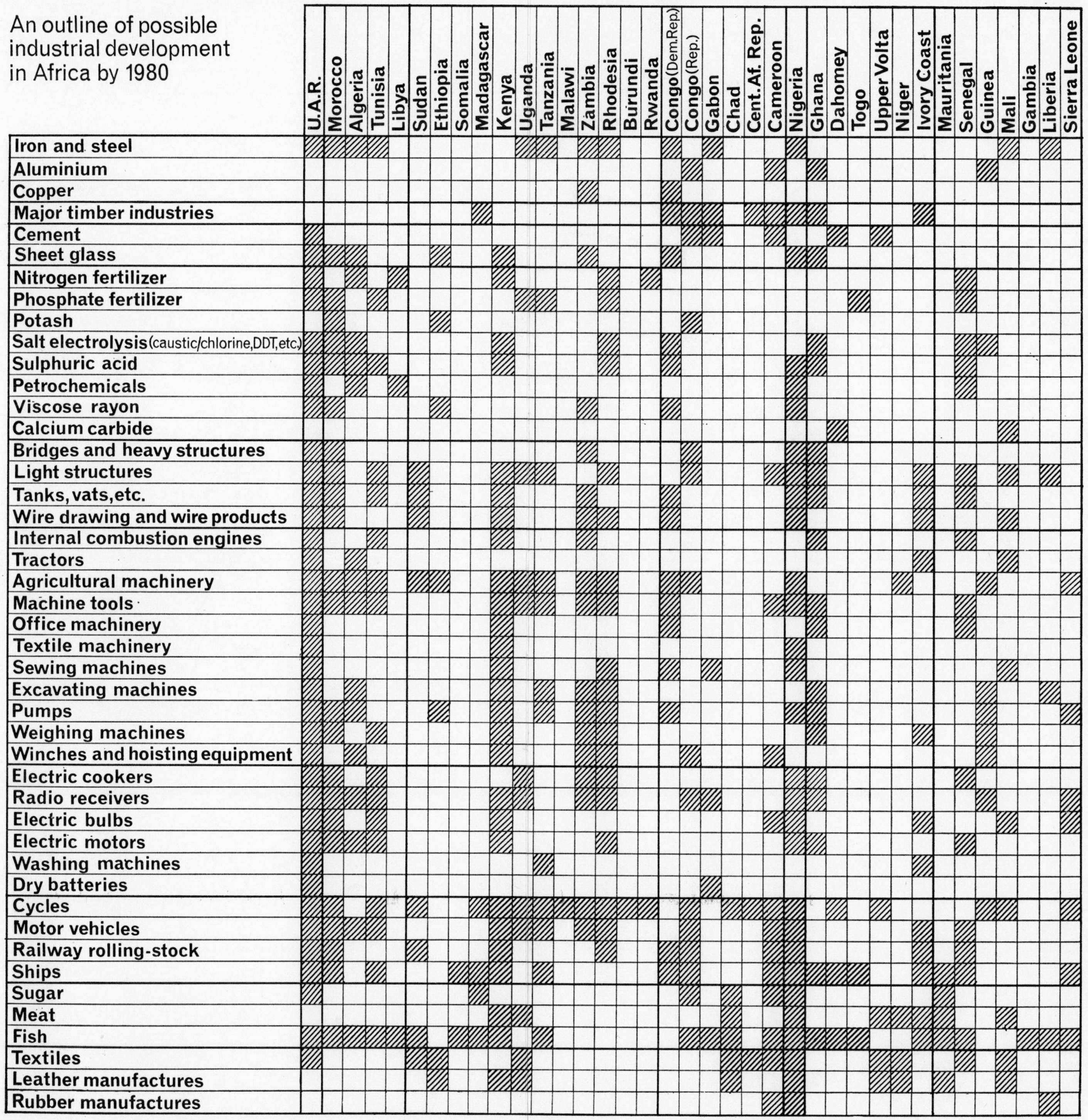

U.A.R.
Morocco
Algeria
Tunisia
Libya
Sudan
Ethiopia
Somalia
Madagascar
Kenya
Uganda
Tanzania
Malawi
Zambia
Rhodesia
Burundi
Rwanda
Congo (Dem. Rep.)
Congo (Rep.)
Gabon
Chad
Cent. Af. Rep.
Cameroon
Nigeria
Ghana
Dahomey
Togo
Upper Volta
Niger
Ivory Coast
Mauritania
Senegal
Guinea
Mali
Gambia
Liberia
Sierra Leone
Iron and steel
Aluminium
Copper
Major timber industries
Cement
Sheet glass
Nitrogen fertilizer
Phosphate fertilizer
Potash
Salt electrolysis (caustic/chlorine, DDT, etc.)
Sulphuric acid
Petrochemicals
Viscose rayon
Calcium carbide
Bridges and heavy structures
Light structures
Tanks, vats, etc.
Wire drawing and wire products
Internal combustion engines
Tractors
Agricultural machinery
Machine tools
Office machinery
Textile machinery
Sewing machines
Excavating machines
Pumps
Weighing machines
Winches and hoisting equipment
Electric cookers
Radio receivers
Electric bulbs
Electric motors
Washing machines
Dry batteries
Cycles
Motor vehicles
Railway rolling-stock
Ships
Sugar
Meat
Fish
Textiles
Leather manufactures
Rubber manufactures

These groupings, at different levels, help to determine the rationale of the industrial location pattern suggested. But their non-exclusive character is highly important. Iron and steel produced in Uganda could be sold in the southern Sudan and eastern Congo. Aluminium and copper products should seek markets well beyond their immediate groupings. The same is partly true of fertilizers. Nitrogen fertilizer which could be produced from Lake Kivu gas could find markets in eastern Congo, Rwanda, Burundi, Uganda, and the southern Sudan. Phosphate fertilizer produced in Togo should find markets in Central Africa. Potash produced in Ethiopia and the Republic of the Congo should find markets all over Africa. Petro-chemicals must also be envisaged on a regional scale, particularly the complex being planned in Algeria. Metal manufactures are being planned mainly on a sub-regional basis or within even smaller groupings. But as progress is made and specialized machinery becomes feasible, thinking will have to be increasingly on a regional scale. There are also cross currents in the major food industries. The francophone African countries south of the Sahara have co-ordinated their sugar programme. The natural channels of trade in meat and meat products are from the hinterland to the coast, cutting right across the groupings, e.g. Mali to Ivory Coast and Chad to Nigeria.

It remains then to try to sum up the potential industrial picture in 1975–80. This is done in a highly simplified form in the chart opposite p. 92.[36] Several points must be stressed. First, the industries shown are confined to those normally requiring the market of two or three, or sometimes several, countries. Hence what may be called purely national industries are omitted. Secondly, some industries are included which are in this category, from the point of view of many African countries, but certainly not all. This applies, for example, to cement and most metal products, which are multi-national industries in some countries but not in others. Thirdly, some groupings adopted are aggregated, e.g. salt electrolysis and machine tools, so that the chart underestimates the range of industries which could be installed. Fourthly, the squares are far from equivalents as between one country and another. The meaning of each square, quantitatively, can be seen from the data given earlier in this chapter.

Even with these evident limitations, the possibilities shown are quite striking, when compared with the existing picture set out in Chapter II.

These, then, are the broad perspectives. They will remain little more than paper fantasies unless the problems which are the principal subject matter of the rest of this book are solved: finance, the prerequisites, and the agents of industrial development.

### A LOOK STILL FURTHER AHEAD

If 1975–80 works out in any way as suggested, it may be legitimate to indulge in further speculation and suggest what might be the situation by the end of the century, in terms of industries laid down.[37] Outline perspectives in general terms were set out at the beginning of this chapter. They may be supplemented by the summary of fairly detailed projections relating to the Maghreb in 1970 and 1990 (measured in milliards of old French francs at 1963 prices):[38]

|  | *1970* | % | *1990* | % | Rate of Growth % |
|---|---|---|---|---|---|
| Agriculture | 815 | 27 | 1,700 | 19 | 3·8 |
| Manufacturing industries: |  |  |  |  |  |
| Basic industries | 120 | 4 | 995 | 11 | 11·2 |
| Light industries | 230 | 8 | 980 | 11 | 7·5 |
| Other sectors | 1,855 | 61 | 5,525 | 60 | 5·6 |
|  | 3,020 | 100 | 9,200 | 100 | 6·0 |

Such a relatively detailed projection seems reasonable in an area where there are serious prospects of the grouping of countries and where there are already dynamic development efforts. Elsewhere, it is too soon to attempt such detail. Yet, if the perspectives for 1975–80 are achieved, it is not pure illusion to suppose that by the end of the century in the region as a whole iron and steel production may be approaching 110 million tons and widely dispersed; that aluminium and copper will be major industries serving markets throughout the continent as well as overseas; that Africa will be a major net exporter of timber manufactures; that cement production will be around 100 million tons; that sulphuric acid production will be about 15 million tons; that there will be several major caustic/chlorine complexes; that production of nitrogen and phosphate fertilizer will be of the order, respectively, of 3 million and 20 million tons; that there will be two or three well-developed petro-chemical complexes providing, *inter alia*, the raw material for a widely dispersed plastics manufactures industry; that metal products will be produced throughout the region; and that mechanical and electrical engineering and transport equipment will be well established in a considerable number of countries, with some of them producing specialized industrial machinery.

By then, although there should be a high degree of industrial self-sufficiency, Africa would be entering into world trade on equal terms and, although still a major exporter of primary products and importer of specialized capital equipment, able to follow the trade patterns of the developed world, so that the main emphasis in the twenty-first century would be exchange of manufactures between Africa and its trading partners overseas.

## NOTES AND REFERENCES TO CHAPTER IV

[1] A study by OECD has suggested that if Italian per capita income were to be compared with that of the United States, it would have to be increased by at least 80 per cent.

[2] J. N. Ypsilantis, 'World and Regional Estimates and Projections of Labour Force', paper prepared for a United Nations Seminar in Elsinore, August 1966.

[3] *Patterns of Industry Growth 1938–1958*, United Nations (Sales No. 59. XVII. 6), New York.

[4] The bulk of the detailed information drawn upon in the remainder of this chapter derives from a whole series of preliminary studies carried out by the ECA, starting with *Industrial Growth in Africa*, op. cit.; the reports of a series of missions designed to open up the way to sub-regional economic co-operation: *Report of the West African Industrial Co-ordination Mission* (E/CN. 14/246); *Report of the ECA Industrial Co-ordination Mission to East Africa* (E/CN. 14/247); *Report of the ECA Industrial Co-ordination Mission to Algeria, Libya, Morocco and Tunisia*, op. cit.; and the *Report of the ECA Mission on Economic Co-operation in Central Africa*, op. cit.; a series of detailed sector studies prepared for a Conference on Industrial Co-operation in West Africa, held in Bamako in 1964; and an even more detailed series of studies prepared for a Conference on Economic Co-operation held in Lusaka in October–November 1965; and finally, a series of sector studies prepared for a Conference on Economic Co-operation in West Africa held in Niamey in October 1966. ECA is also working out, with the aid of approximate input–output tables, industrial balance sheets relating to 1980 and beyond, for the different sub-regions of Africa. (Cf. H. B. Chenery and P. G. Clark, *Interindustry Economics*, Wiley, New York, 1959, p. 333: 'We suggest that further development of interindustry methods should concentrate on the uses for which this approach shows a real advantage over alternative techniques.

H

These are problems which involve a pronounced departure from previous trends in one or more parts of the economy.')The general approach adopted here, although based largely on ECA material, is not necessarily in accordance with ECA's conclusions, which indeed, as will be seen, cannot be expected to take final shape until the industrial balance studies are completed in, it is expected, the first half of 1968.

⁵ The share of construction in gross domestic fixed capital formation in selected countries is as follows: Federal Republic of Germany and United Kingdom, 45; France, 47; Rhodesia and Nyasaland, 53; Kenya, 58; United States, 64; Ghana, 71. The share of construction in GDP normally varies from 3 to 6 per cent and accounts for between 8 and 14 per cent of total employment (see *The Construction Industry in Development Programmes: A Techno-economic Review in the West African Sub-region*, document E/CN. 14/INR/107, Addis Ababa, July 1966).

⁶ *The Iron and Steel Industry in Africa*, ECA (E/CN. 14/AS/III/23), Addis Ababa, December 1965.

⁷ See *Long Term Trends and Problems of the European Steel Industry*, ECE (Sales No. 60. II. E.3), Geneva, 1959.

⁸ See document E/CN. 14/INR/87, July 1965, prepared for the ECA by W. S. Atkins and Partners, and Add. 2, prepared by the ECA secretariat.

⁹ See *Report of the ECA Mission on Economic Co-operation in Central Africa*, op. cit., Chap. V(e).

¹⁰ See *Iron and Steel and the First Stage of Transformation*, prepared for ECA by SETEC and Prof. de Bernis and associates (E/CN. 14/INR/72), Vols I and II, Addis Ababa, July 1964, and also Addendum on Mauritania, prepared by SETEC, May 1965.

¹¹ An independent estimate in a feasibility study commissioned by the Liberian Government arrived at a virtually identical figure.

¹² *Competition between Steel and Aluminium*, ECE (E/ECE/184), Geneva, 1954. A similar conclusion based on up-to-date data can be found in *Africa and the Aluminium Industry*, Appendix B, prepared for the ECA by S. Moment, 1965.

¹³ See Chapter II.

¹⁴ The limited immediate possibilities of producing aluminium metal in West and Central Africa, as seen by an expert from Pechiney, and the shifting centre of gravity in the location of the world aluminium industry are set out in *Rapport sur l'industrie de l'aluminium dans la zone centrale et ouest de l'Afrique* (document E/CN. 14/INR/137), Addis Ababa, September 1966.

¹⁵ See *Africa and the Aluminium Industry*, op. cit., p. 4.

¹⁶ See *Report of the ECA Industrial Co-ordination Mission to East Africa*, ECA (E/CN. 14 /247), Addis Ababa, December 1963, para. 59.

¹⁷ See *Report of the ECA/FAO Economic Survey Mission on the Economic Development of Zambia*, N'Dola, 1964.

¹⁸ See *Timber Trends and Prospects in Africa*, FAO/ECA, Rome, 1965.

¹⁹ See *European Timber Trends and Prospects, A New Appraisal, 1950–1975*, UN/FAO, New York, 1964.

²⁰ See *Report of FAO/ECAFE Conference on Pulp and Paper Development Prospects in Asia and the Far East*, Tokyo, 1960. See also *Proceedings and Related Papers of the Conference on Pulp and Paper Developments in Africa and the Near East*, Cairo, 1965.

[21] See *Development of Forest Industries in Africa*, FAO (E/CN. 14/AS/III/3). This paper *inter alia* sets out a summary programme of action.

[22] *Development of Forest Industries in Africa*, op. cit., p. 53.

[23] *A Review of the Building Materials Industry in Africa*, ECA (E/CN. 14/AS/III/5), Addis Ababa, December 1965.

[24] *A Review of the Building Materials Industry in Africa*, op. cit., p. 26.

[25] See *The Building Materials Industry in Africa. Present Situation and Future Prospects*, ECA (HOU/WP/4), 1963. See also *A Review of the Building Materials Industry in Africa*, op. cit.

[26] See *A Review of the Building Materials Industry in Africa*, op. cit., p. 28.

[27] The main sources drawn upon are:

*Basic Chemicals and Fertilizers in West Africa*, prepared for the ECA by the Battelle Institute (E/CN. 14/INR/73), 1964.

*Investigations on Fertilizer and Chemical Industries in East Africa*, prepared for the ECA by the Battelle Institute (E/CN. 14/INR/83), 1965.

*Report of the ECA Mission on Economic Co-operation in Central Africa*, op. cit., Chap. VII (h).

*Prospects for the Development of the Chemical Industry in Africa* (E/CN. 14/AS/III/22), 1965.

There is some overlapping in these documents and specific reference to them (and other sources) is made only where strictly necessary. Reference should also be made to an unpublished study made available to the writer by the Institut de science économique appliquée, Dakar, concerning the Senegal River Basin countries; and to an ingenious and imaginative sketch of chemical industry development possibilities in *An Outline Survey of Possible Industrial Opportunities in the Rhodesias and Nyasaland*, prepared in 1963 by the Federal Ministry of Commerce and Industry—too late, of course, to save the Federation.

[28] See *Prospects for the Development of the Chemical Industry in Africa*, op. cit., Table 7.

[29] See in this connection *Soil Fertility and Fertilizers in West Africa*, prepared by Dr. E. W. Hauck, FAO (E/CN. 14/INR/70 Rev. 1). This is a revision by the author of a document prepared two years earlier and shows a considerable increase in the consumption forecast.

[30] See *Report of the ECA Mission on Economic Co-operation in Central Africa*, op. cit., Chap. VII (h), and J. Depardieu, '*Essai de comparaison technico-économique de divers engrais*', *Chimie et Industries*, Vol. 93, No. 4, April 1965.

[31] For a discussion of what has been and can be done, see *Soil Fertility and Fertilizers in West Africa*, op. cit.

[32] The sources drawn upon are: the *Reports of the ECA Industrial Co-ordination Missions;* the *Report of the ECA Mission on Economic Co-operation in Central Africa*, op. cit., Chap. VII (f); *The Development of the Engineering Industries in East Africa—Mechanical Engineering* (E/CN. 14/INR/90); *Electro-technical Engineering Industries in the East African Sub-region* (E/CN. 14/INR/89); *Engineering Industries in Africa* (E/CN. 14/INR/AS/II/2.1); and *Iron and Steel and the First Stage of Transformation*, op. cit., Vol. II.

[33] *Report of the ECA Industrial Co-ordination Mission to Algeria, Libya, Morocco and Tunisia*, op. cit., p. 137.

³⁴ *Textile Industries in Africa*, ECA (E/CN. 14/AS/III/24), Addis Ababa, 1966.

³⁵ See Chapter VI.

³⁶ Much more detailed estimates, including virtually the whole range of industry, multi-national and national, with quantitative targets, estimates of investment, employment, etc., as part of an attempt to propound balanced over-all sub-regional industrial development programmes, have been proposed by the ECA for East and for Central Africa and are in preparation for West and for North Africa. See *Industrial Co-ordination in East Africa: A Quantified Approach to First Approximations* (E/CN. 14/INR/102), and *Report of the ECA Mission on Economic Co-operation in Central Africa*, op. cit., Chap. VII.

³⁷ See A. F. Ewing and S. J. Patel, *Perspectives for Industrialization in Africa*, from which what follows is partly drawn. A reviewer in *Nature* (15 February 1966) described this paper as 'science fiction', perhaps not wholly without just-ice, since it was concerned only with perspectives and left out the 'how', which is the main theme of this book. But given that the 'how' can be solved, the present writer remains unrepentant about the levels of industrialization which can be achieved in Africa by the turn of the century.

³⁸ Samir Amin, *L'Économie du Maghreb* , op. cit., Vol. II, concluding chapter, and particularly p. 211.

CHAPTER V

# TRADE AND INTEGRATION

It has been shown in an earlier chapter that African countries depend heavily on foreign trade, which accounts for about a quarter of GDP. This is mainly trade between Africa and the rest of the world, exchange of primary products against manufactures and semi-manufactures. Intra-African trade accounts for less than 10 per cent of total trade and is mainly exchange of primary products.

The relatively limited scope for increased export of primary products, except for some minerals, was pointed out in Chapter I. There is scope for a higher degree of processing of primary products for export. But the only real way to increase African trade is by more intra-African trade. To some extent this can be facilitated by reduction of tariff and other trade barriers, better trading mechanisms, and harmonization of payments arrangements. Transport deficiencies are examined later; the relevant point here is that if new links among African countries are to be viable, there will have to be a large increase in the volume of goods to be transported.

All the arguments lead to the same conclusion. Intra-African trade is limited because nearly all African countries produce the same few products. If trade is to be increased, there will have to be available more tradeable goods, which means diversification of the economies and thus extensive industrialization. In African conditions, industrialization is impossible without increased trade among neighbours. Specific provision for trade expansion has to be made in national development plans.[1] Progressive economic co-operation is essential, with steady progress towards economic integration.

In discussing movements towards regional integration, a clear distinction has to be made between already developed and developing regions.[2] The experience of Western Europe has shown that where there is a group of economies at a high and reasonably comparable level of per capita income, fairly rapid progress can be made towards the lowering of trade barriers against industrial

99

goods, with a beneficial effect on total industrial output, productivity, and the volume of trade. A virtual customs union in industrial goods was attained in the EEC as far back as 1959 and some
progress has been made somewhat later in the countries of the
EFTA. On the other hand, the prolonged crisis in the EEC over
agriculture has shown all too clearly that even advanced countries
are not prepared to adopt a similar approach for farm products.
The Six have now established a strongly State-directed and highly
protected system of organized agricultural markets. The EFTA has
left agriculture entirely out of its system. What this means is that
even advanced countries are not prepared to leave their farming
interests to the mercy of market forces, but that, given always a
high degree of industrial development and limited differences in
levels of development among countries, market forces under free
trade conditions can be beneficial. It should be added that even in
Europe there are less favoured pockets and that special steps have
had to be taken to deal with them, through deliberate State or
inter-state intervention against the normal play of the market.

Turning now to the problem of regional integration in developing areas, the first point which emerges is that, *a fortiori*, there is
still less reason to expect a free-trade/common-market approach in
agriculture, since in addition to the arguments applicable in advanced countries, agriculture accounts for a much larger proportion of total output and the peasant producer's standard of living
is already so low that to expose him to further competition would
be politically and socially disastrous.[3] In the case of industrial
products four main problems arise, particularly in African conditions. The first is that the volume and range of industrial production is so limited that free trade in itself is not likely to make a great
deal of difference. The second is that there are marked differences
among countries in the competitive power of such industry as is
already installed, so that it is natural and inevitable that the
weaker should wish to protect what little they have. This argument
is greatly reinforced by the fact that since industry is largely in
foreign hands and inevitably tends to gravitate to established locations, the threat to the poorer areas is so much the greater. The
third point is that, unlike advanced countries, the industrial map is
relatively empty and thus the task is not to free trade in what
exists so much as to build up, on a joint basis, new industry. In
arriving at such agreements for multi-national industry, it would,

of course, be absurd to set up trading barriers between the partners. But the emphasis is on the deliberate creation on a joint basis
of new industry, and in doing this attention has to be paid throughout to locating a sufficient proportion of the new industry in the
poorer areas, even though in some cases it can be shown that
ideally, in terms of the total rate of growth, other locations might
be preferable. The fourth is, of course, limitations in existing transport networks.

There are four relevant experiences of approaches to regional
integration from other developing areas: Asia, Central America,
South America, and Eastern Europe.[4]

Asia is relevant in this context, in the first instance primarily in
terms of the efforts of the ECAFE secretariat, and especially an
aide-mémoire drawn up in 1955 by its first Executive Secretary,
P. S. Lokanathan, on regional co-operation. This aide-mémoire
drew attention to the limitations of national economic planning,
the scope for inter-governmental co-operation in specific fields,
e.g. the development of the Mekong River, where subsequently
some progress has been made, and the need to associate the various
international initiatives in the region more closely together.[5] It is
argued that the subsequent efforts of ECAFE and all the relevant
moves towards regional co-operation in Asia have derived from
this aide-mémoire. It is also shown that ECAFE has been responsible for a significant programme of economic co-operation in
specific, if limited, economic and technical fields. More recently,
ECAFE has been responsible for the establishment of an Asian
Development Bank. Nevertheless, little has been done towards
economic co-operation in Asia in the sense of mutually concerted
development programmes, especially in industry. This is hardly
surprising, and for three reasons. First, the geographical factor, the
lack of land frontiers and the vast distances which have to be
covered by sea or air. Secondly, the political differences among
Asian countries are more acute than in Africa or Latin America.
Thirdly, the disparities in economic configuration and degree of
development are enormous, from Japan (now a developed country
by any standards), through India and China (very large territories
which, in different ways, have made progress towards development), to relatively small and backward countries such as Thai-
land, Laos, and Cambodia.

Central America comprises five small countries: El Salvador,

Guatemala, Honduras, Nicaragua, and Costa Rica, with a total population of 13 million, with low incomes per head (although relatively high by African standards), and depending mainly on exports of agricultural commodities to world markets, coffee, cotton, cocoa, and bananas accounting for 90 per cent of their exports.[6]

The efforts towards integration in Central America are of particular interest for Africa in view of the small size of the countries and their economic structure. A general treaty on Central American economic integration was signed in Managua in December 1960. Under this treaty the signatory states agreed to grant to one another free-trade treatment with respect to all products originating in their respective territories, with limited exceptions. The intention was, apart from the exceptions, unrestricted free trade at the end of five years. It was recognized that real development depends on inward-directed growth and that, given the total size of the market in the five countries, industrial specialization was essential. It was also recognized that while private enterprise must be the main motor, the governments concerned had an important part to play.

The early agreements concerned 'integration industries' in limited consumer and some intermediate goods. The range was not impressive but none the less an improvement on the totally uncoordinated development in first-stage industry in the small countries of South America. There was scant recognition of the need to move forward towards intermediate and capital goods. On the other hand, the earlier failures have led to some rethinking, notably a meeting in May 1965 which drew attention to the economic feasibility of some seventy new industrial projects.[7]

Limited as may have been the progress so far in Central America it is perhaps the best pointer yet to what may be done in Africa, and more positive than that of South America.

Most of the South American countries signed an agreement for a free-trade area (LAFTA) at Montevideo in 1960.[8] The LAFTA treaty provided for freeing of trade covering 25 per cent of trade among the countries concerned during the first three years, trade which was mainly in primary products. Nevertheless, great difficulties were experienced in finding a common list of items, suggesting that to move on to further stages, as laid down in the treaty—50 per cent, 75 per cent, and 100 per cent—would be still

harder. The reason for these difficulties, the fact that efforts towards liberalization were based on existing patterns of trade,
mainly in primary commodities, is hardly surprising in the light of
the general considerations set out earlier in this chapter.[9] As Dell
argues:

> Economic integration will not give Latin America an easy road to
> higher living standards or render unnecessary the painful adjustments
> that the political and social circumstances of the region have shown to
> be necessary. It can increase the power of the economic forces of de-
> velopment once those forces are well and truly mobilized. It can never
> substitute for them.

He brings out not so much the conflict between, as the complementarity of, nationalism and continentalism, and shows that a
movement towards a free-trade area or common market based on
existing economic structures makes limited sense only, that integration is primarily relevant within the context of harmonized development of new industries, and that this requires much more
than the creation of a milieu for the promotion of market forces,
but rather a conscious inter-state directed effort.

It has been shown in an earlier chapter that the easy stage of
import substitution in Latin America has been largely attained and
and that further growth depends either on breaking into world
markets for manufactures or an integrated programme within
Latin America of production of intermediate and capital goods. It
has been pointed out that

> the fields on which ECLA most enthusiastically set its eyes for future
> integrated Latin American projects are steel, aluminium, branches of
> the chemical industry (like fertilizers, sodium alkalis and the basic petro-
> chemical industry), pulp and paper, the manufacture of basic capital
> equipment (for the production of steel and petroleum, the generation
> of electric power and the manufacture of pulp and paper), transport
> material (for road, rail and water transport), machine tools, textile
> machinery and road building equipment.[10]

It is in this range of industry that lie the real relevance and potential of LAFTA. Yet the obstacles are formidable, as has been shown
recently.[11] These are the big agricultural interests oriented towards
markets in the industrial countries, established manufacturers of
consumer goods living a comfortable life behind high protective
tariffs, inefficient small entrepreneurs, and international industrial

firms. All these interests are doing very well now, but they are contributing virtually nothing to the economic development of Latin America.

In principle, economic co-operation and eventually economic integration among fully planned socialist economies should be easier than among markets or mixed economies. In practice, the Eastern European countries have been making much progress, but there have been difficulties to overcome and the lessons are instructive for Africa.[12] The first phase of economic co-operation lasted until the end of 1948 and was of limited significance, amounting to a simple exchange of surpluses. The Council for Mutual Economic Assistance was established in January 1949 and began the second phase. During this period, which lasted until the beginning of 1956, the only real link was a series of long-term trade agreements. In national development plans each country went its own way and there was a tendency to autarchy. As a result, intra-Eastern European trade began to stagnate. In the third and current phase an international division of labour began to be worked out and steps taken towards economic integration. But the Eastern European bloc is far from being a single economic entity.

By the middle of the 1950s the structure of foreign exchange had begun to change in such a way that the formerly less-developed countries of the region exported less raw materials and more machinery while the more advanced countries began to import more machinery from their neighbours. However, the earlier attempts at integration during the second phase were largely frustrated since the recommendations worked out by the COMECON were on a technological rather than an economic basis. During this period, excessive autarchy was sharply criticized. It was recognized that this tendency was based mainly on industry and in particular capital goods whereas extraction industries and agriculture were being neglected. In the discussions leading to the third phase it was recognized that productivity and economic viability were the main criteria. It began to be recognized that there was considerable scope for international specialization in the production of intermediate goods—iron and steel, non-ferrous metals, heavy chemicals, and building materials—on the basis of comparative advantage in natural resource endowment. It was also recognized that manufacturing, and in particular engineering, had to be developed in all countries. In the field of consumer goods it was agreed that there should be a wide assortment of final products in every country, but that there was much scope for international specialization and exchange in terms of types, brands, and designs. Thus the third phase of co-operation began to get under way, not through any attempt to establish centralized planning machinery for the whole region so much as by progressive co-ordination of national economic plans. In fact much of the co-operation established was on the basis of joint efforts by two or more countries. This type of approach has been facilitated by the absence of private ownership.

The third period shows many examples of successful joint ventures, e.g. joint efforts by Czechoslovakia and Poland in the development of the Polish coal mines, copper mines, and sulphur deposits; a joint approach to the development of potash fertilizers in the USSR and Eastern Germany; joint exploitation of Romanian cellulose and manufacturing of paper, and extensive efforts for the harnessing and distribution of water power, oil, and natural gas resources. The long-distance transmission of oil and natural gas is of particular importance in relation to the development, on a co-ordinated but widely dispersed basis, of petro-chemicals.

Apart from petro-chemicals, international specialization in the chemical industry and in particular traditional inorganic chemicals has not proved to be easy. However, in the most recent phase, much has been done to co-ordinate and specialize in the production of chemical equipment. Similarly, co-operation and specialization in the production of mechanical, electrical, and transport equipment has also proved difficult. For example, little progress has been made in the motor-vehicle field largely because there were established interests at the beginning of the period. Bearing in mind also the proliferation of assembly of motor vehicles in Latin America and also to some extent North Africa, this experience is fraught with lessons for Africa. On the other hand, co-ordination and specialization in production of roller and ball-bearings has been fruitful. Out of some 2,200 types required about 500 are now being manufactured in two or more countries and the rest in one country with, of course, beneficial results in the field of trade. In the whole field of specialized production of equipment, as distinct from the general run of mechanical and electrical engineering, the Eastern European experience has shown that there is much scope for international specialization, e.g. oil extraction equipment in Romania and the USSR; oil refining equipment in Czechoslovakia, Romania, and the USSR; small section rolling mills in Eastern Germany and in Poland; large section rolling mills in Czechoslovakia and the USSR; wire-drawing mills in Eastern Germany and Hungary; cement equipment in Eastern Germany, Poland, and the USSR; paper-manufacturing equipment in Czechoslovakia, Eastern Germany, and Poland; electric arc furnaces in Poland and the USSR; excavators in Czechoslovakia, Eastern Germany, and the USSR; electric cars and agricultural machinery in Bulgaria; and electrical equipment, buses, and food industry equipment in Hungary.

Africa is at least a decade away from production of specialized machinery, yet the Eastern European thesis that it is a major aim to lay down in as many countries as possible mechanical and electrical engineering and, as a prior stage, metal products, is well worth pondering. So also is the scope for international specialization in production of raw materials and energy.

Despite the interesting perspectives, the experience of regional integration in other developing areas is not particularly encouraging, although both the reasons why and what could be the appropriate approach are clear. The need for a regional, or rather a subregional, approach in Africa is much stronger than elsewhere, owing to the very small size of so many African countries. The opportunities are also greater, owing to the level of development and therefore the limited significance of existing vested interests which militate against economic co-operation. The next step, therefore, is to examine briefly what has been or is being done.

Partly as a result of a preliminary inquiry carried out by the ECA,[13] a serious start has been made in the four countries of the Maghreb. An institutional structure has been set up with a ministerial commission, technical commissions, and a permanent secretariat. The technical commissions cover industry, trade, transport, posts and telecommunications, tourism, statistics, and national accounts. The commission for industry has so far been sub-divided into sub-commissions for iron and steel, assembly industries, glass, and electrical industries.[14] Studies on the industrial branches concerned are in progress and it is only fair to add that while there has been much discussion and negotiation, agreements have yet to be arrived at. The difficulties are due partly to the fact that there are already a fair degree of industrial development in

North Africa and therefore established vested interests standing in the way of industrial harmonization. The fact remains that there are, within the Maghreb, the beginnings of a genuine understanding as to the need for co-operation, particularly in the industrial field, and that the institutional arrangements already established and at work suggest that genuine progress can be expected in the next two or three years.

There have been vicissitudes in East Africa. When the three ex-British territories, Tanzania, Uganda, and Kenya, became independent, there were high hopes of an East African Federation, which have subsequently faded, and the common market in these territories was beginning to break up, notably through the establishment of separate currencies, national central banks, and the setting up of trade barriers among the three countries.

It is now clear that there were always illusions about the degree of integration in British East Africa, which were in fact analysed in 1963 at a time when general opinion was still relatively optimistic and thinking in terms of federation.[15] It was pointed out that although economic integration was more advanced in East Africa than among other African countries, there was no provision, as in the Treaty of Rome, for improvement in the mobility of labour and capital, no forward schedule of stages in the advance towards fuller integration, no common judicial body, and a weak bureaucracy. The EACSO (East African Common Services Organization) and related services were concerned largely with infrastructure. Furthermore, the most important point, the three countries had grown at unequal rates and industry tended to gravitate particularly towards Kenya, especially Nairobi and Mombasa. By 1958, of 474 companies registered in East Africa, 404 were in Kenya. A World Bank mission to Tanzania argued that 'from the point of view of Tanzania, an argument may be made for some measure of infant industry protection, not only against imports from overseas but against imports from other members of the Customs Union, and in particular Kenya'.[16] Another inquiry about the same period concluded that although Tanzania had suffered, on balance, no absolute disadvantage from the common market, it had not benefited.[17]

The most recent analysis[18] aggregates the gains and losses in terms of the common market in industry and partially in agriculture, the Common Services, and fiscal transfers. It is estimated that

Kenya gained £18·5 million, Uganda £0·8 million, and that Tanzania lost £4·1 million. The main sources of gains were the Common Services. The common market in industry would have been more fruitful if there had in fact been more industries installed requiring the whole market (which under the then prevailing conditions would probably have increased Kenya's gains). The Raisman fiscal redistribution formula has been a failure. But the final conclusion is that the cost of breaking up the whole system would be formidable and hence the right answer is to reorganize, and this is what is in fact being done.

A Commission (the Philips Commission) was set up and, as a result of its report and subsequent negotiations, a new Treaty has been signed. The common external tariff will remain, but, to encourage industrial development in the less-favoured areas, a transfer tax of up to 50 per cent of the equivalent external customs tariffs imposed on the relevant goods coming from outside East Africa, subject to conditions laid down in the Treaty, may be imposed by any country on manufactured products from its neighbours.[19] The three countries are setting up a joint development bank. The Common Services will be maintained, but as four public corporations operating on a profit-making basis. Attempts are also now being made to establish a system of economic co-operation on a wider, yet looser, basis in the whole eastern African subregion, from Ethiopia in the north to Tanzania and the former members of the Federation of Rhodesia and Nyasaland in the south, and Rwanda and Burundi in the west. Following a conference on Economic Co-operation in East Africa held in Lusaka in October–November 1965, largely devoted to industrial questions, a meeting was held in Addis Ababa in May 1966 at ministerial level, at which a number of East African countries decided to establish an East African economic community, subject to the drawing up of a detailed treaty and later ratification.[20] The machinery envisaged provides for a permanent ministerial council and standing technical bodies, together with a permanent secretariat. It will be some time before this community comes into operation. Furthermore, the real substance of negotiations about harmonization of sectors of the East African economy, and in particular industry, remains for the future.[21]

In Central Africa there are six countries, the four former members of French Equatorial Africa, which, together with the Cameroon, are now party to the Treaty of UDEAC, and the Democratic Republic of the Congo. The Treaty of UDEAC came into force at the beginning of 1966. It provides for a customs union, a common external tariff, detailed harmonization of fiscal policies and investment incentives, and standing machinery at both the ministerial and technical level.[22] Although there is in principle provision for harmonization of industrial policies and programmes, little has yet been done, partly owing to the fact that the institutional machinery for industrial development remains at the present stage weak and, perhaps more important, because the economies of these countries are still largely dependent on external forces. A further problem is that so far little or no effort has been made to arrive at agreements for economic co-operation between the UDEAC countries and the Democratic Republic of the Congo. Such agreements will be by no means easy to arrive at, partly owing to the fact that the development of the Democratic Republic of the Congo has been greater than the UDEAC countries taken together, and partly owing to currency and payments problems.

Next there is West Africa, consisting of fourteen countries of different sizes and degrees of development and divided between countries with different histories, institutions, cultures, and languages. Efforts have been made, largely through the ECA, to provide a basis for a common industrial development programme, and these continue.[23] A conference held in Niamey in October 1966 accepted the general principles of a West African economic community along the same lines as that agreed upon in Lusaka a year earlier for East Africa.

In practice, there would seem to be two focal points for possible future agreements of a more detailed character. One is the so-called *Entente*, the loose grouping of French-speaking states led by the Ivory Coast, comprising also Niger, Upper Volta, Dahomey, and Togo. This arrangement consists of a customs union, and a mutual loan and guarantee fund, a device concerned to compensate for the fact that there is a marked difference in the degree of development of the Ivory Coast and the other countries.[24] So far, the Entente can hardly be regarded as a serious effort towards economic integration, mainly owing to the marked inequality between the Ivory Coast and its small and impoverished partners. On the other hand, recent political events in Ghana may make it possible for the hitherto almost impregnable barriers between this country and the

Entente to be broken down, If such proves to be the case, there could be the nucleus of a viable economic grouping in this part of West Africa.

There remain the four countries associated with the Senegal River Basin: Guinea, Mali, Mauritania, and Senegal. Largely under the impetus of projects heavily supported by the United Nations Development Programme to develop the Senegal River Basin for irrigation, energy, and navigation, a Council of Ministers has been established, together with standing technical bodies and a permanent secretariat. A study is in progress, going well beyond the development of the river basin, aiming at the co-ordinated economic development and eventual integration of these four countries. The key factor is industry and, as has been pointed out in Chapter IV, these prospects are not unpromising, at least in economic terms.

Lastly, a word should be said about the association between eighteen African countries (mainly French-speaking) and the EEC through the Yaounde Convention. These African countries obtain preferences for their agricultural exports in the markets of the Six and significant financial aid. In return, the Six obtain preferences for their industrial products in the markets of the eighteen countries. There are also joint institutions. It has been argued that these arrangements tend to inhibit African industrial development, and especially sub-regional arrangements for joint development with non-associated countries. In the Convention, protection of infant industries, including sub-regional arrangements with non-associated countries, seems to be admissible, but in practice this apparently remains to be tested.

In the recent Nigerian agreement with the EEC, there are no joint institutions and no provision for financial aid. Nigerian exports will have free entry into the markets of the Six, but some of the most important, e.g. cocoa, palm oil, and plywood, will only enter duty-free in amounts equal to the average imports of the Six from 1962 to 1964, with a small subsequent annual increase. Nigeria has opened her market to EEC products to only a very limited extent.

The Yaounde Convention expires in 1968 and it is not too soon to think of future arrangements. The Nigerian model may prove to be a useful one, particularly if it can become applicable on an all-African non-discriminatory scale.[25] The essence of the EEC's attraction at this stage is its significant financial aid to its members, both for budget support and investment projects. The basic principles of the Convention of Association are grounded in reciprocity, exactly the opposite of current, post-UNCTAD thinking on aid. Financial assistance is necessary, but it should surely be divorced from commercial concessions exacted from African countries.[26]

## NOTES AND REFERENCES TO CHAPTER V

[1] For an analysis in this respect of eight African development plans and the contrast in planning foreign trade between inward and externally propelled development, e.g. the UAR and Tunisia, and Ethiopia and Nigeria, respectively, see *Foreign Trade Plans in Selected Countries in Africa*, ECA Secretariat (E/Conf. 46/83), Addis Ababa, March 1964.

[2] Cf. J. H. Mensah, 'Regional Economic Integration' in *Planning the External Sector: techniques, problems and policies*, United Nations (Sales No. 67. II. B.5), New York, 1967.

[3] This is not to say that among groups of African countries there is not scope for some specialization in agriculture, but if this is to work it will have to be deliberately organized.

[4] There is a vast and growing literature on economic integration. Much of it derives from or is around the experiences of the EEC. Much has also been written about Latin America, the original sources being the work of the ECLA secretariat. There is also an increasing literature on African problems, much of it from the ECA secretariat. This study is not primarily concerned with problems of integration. Some of the original sources are cited in their context of industrial development. Two other works should be mentioned. One is Bela Belassa, *The Theory of Economic Integration*, R. D. Irwin, Illinois, 1961; a primarily theoretical work inspired particularly by European experience, which has also a full bibliography. The other is Sidney Dell, *Trade Blocs and Common Markets*, London, 1963, which, although also theoretical in conception and based particularly on European experience, has also something important to say about the developing areas.

[5] See D. Wightman, *Towards Economic Cooperation in Asia*, New Haven and London, 1963.

[6] The original sources on the problems of Central America are the ECLA secretariat and these are cited in detail in the work drawn upon in the present context, namely: M. S. Wionczek, *The Experiences of the Central American Economic Integration Programme as applied to East Africa*, United Nations (CID/SYMP. B/12), New York, December 1965; J. C. Mills, 'Development Policy and Regional Trading Arrangements', *Economic Development and Cultural Change*, Vol. XIII, No. 1, October 1964; and Sidney Dell, *A Latin American Common Market?*, London, 1966, Chapter IV.

I

[7] M. S. Wionczek, op. cit., p. 16.

[8] The original sources are the treaty documents reproduced in Sidney Dell, *A Latin American Common Market?*, op. cit., Appendices, for texts, and the ECLA secretariat documents; for commentary and analysis, see Dell, ibid., and Wionczek, op. cit.

[9] See also Sidney Dell, *A Latin American Common Market?*, op. cit., Chap. XII.

[10] *The Economist*, 25 September–1 October 1965.

[11] M. S. Wionczek, op. cit.

[12] This account is based mainly on *Economic Integration and Industrial Specialization among Member Countries of the Council for Mutual Economic Assistance*, United Nations (Sales No. 66. II. B.4), New York, 1966.

[13] See the *Report of the ECA Industrial Co-ordination Mission to Algeria, Libya, Morocco and Tunisia*, op. cit.

[14] See *Economic Co-operation in North Africa*, a note prepared by the North African sub-regional office of ECA (E/CN. 14/CA/ECOP/2), February 1966.

[15] J. S. Nye, 'East African Economic Integration', *Journal of Modern African Studies*, Vol. 1., No. 4.

[16] IBRD, *The Economic Development of Tanzania*, pp. 133–4.

[17] The Drees Mission, ECA, Addis Ababa, 1962.

[18] See R. H. Green, *Economic Community in East Africa: A Quantitative Appraisal* (to be published).

[19] See Treaty for East African Co-operation, Nairobi, 1967.

[20] See *Report of the Interim Council of Ministers of the proposed Economic Community of Eastern Africa* (E/CN. 14/352), Addis Ababa.

[21] At this stage, it seems unnecessary to dwell on the failures of the former Federation of Rhodesia and Nyasaland, a common market comprising three countries, Rhodesia, Zambia, and Malawi, which blatantly operated in favour of one country, Rhodesia. For an account of what happened, of why in fact on purely economic grounds the Federation broke up, see *Report of the ECA/FAO Economic Survey Mission on the Economic Development of Zambia*, op. cit., Chap. I.

[22] See *Report of the ECA Mission on Economic Co-operation in Central Africa*, op. cit., Chaps. I and VIII.

[23] Efforts in the case of iron and steel have been described in Chapter IV.

[24] For the latest arrangements recently agreed, see *West Africa*, June 1966.

[25] Cf. A. Rivkin, 'Africa and the EEC', *Finance and Development*, Vol. III, No. 2, 1966.

[26] Cf. J. H. Mensah, 'Regional Economic Integration', op. cit.

# CHAPTER VI

# CAPITAL FORMATION

Any discussion of the financing of industrial development must necessarily examine the whole problem of capital formation from both domestic and foreign sources. Much, too much, current discussion is focused on the external aid problem, and in this chapter the emphasis will be placed more on possibilities of mobilizing and deploying domestic savings. There is no pretension here to examine in depth so vast a subject. The main objective is to put the financing of industrial development and what can be done about it into perspective and to show that finance is not the major constraint.

In order to establish the orders of magnitude of the capital required it is convenient to start from the quantitative estimates which have been made within the context of discussions on aid policy. The case for capital aid has been put in its starkest terms by the United Nations Secretariat.[1] It is projected that a 4·8 per cent average growth in the GDP of the under-developed countries as a whole would give rise to annual import requirements which would be 95 per cent higher in 1970 than in 1959. Export receipts from the sale of primary products at constant prices are expected to rise by only 40 per cent. Accordingly the current trade gap with developed countries, after taking into account a projected US $2 million increase in the export of manufactures, would rise by US $11 milliard, and the balance of payments gap on current account, on the assumption that the net adverse balance on invisible account would increase by US $4 million, would rise by US $15 milliard. In round figures the gap increases therefore from US $5 milliard in 1959 to US $20 milliard in 1970, without making any allowance for amortization of past debts. The consequence of these calculations in terms of increase in net aid, that is to say over and above debt repayments, is more than twice the (then) projected growth rate of the national income of the advanced countries. Projected still further forward to 1980, the balance of payments gap rises to US $57 milliard.

It is familiar and has already been pointed out that the prospects of a growth of export of primary products other than metals from the under-developed to the developed countries are far from good; that there is some hope of a significant contribution through an increase in exports of primary products to the Eastern European countries; and that much hope is now being placed on the export to advanced countries of manufactures, although this applies particularly to Latin America and some Asian countries rather than to Africa. These calculations are valid without making any assumptions as to whether the terms of trade will worsen or improve from the point of view of the under-developed countries.

A calculation has been made[2] of a hypothetical character, attempting to put into perspective the whole problem of how the current balance of payments of the under-developed countries might move in the next forty years. It is assumed that imports increase by 6 per cent a year, a necessary consequence of a growth rate of GDP of 5 per cent. It is assumed that exports of primary products to the developed countries increase by 3 per cent and by 9 per cent to the countries of Eastern Europe, and that exports of manufactures increase by 10 per cent. It is further assumed that the terms of trade remain constant and that the average interest is 3 per cent. On these assumptions the trade gap expressed as a percentage of imports begins to diminish after 1980 and the balance of payments gap after 1990, although in absolute terms the latter continues to rise until the year 2000. The cumulative deficit in the balance of payments up to the year 2000 is US $1,366 milliard, an almost inconceivable sum but no greater than the 1·5 per cent of the GNP of the developed countries over the period, assuming a growth rate of 4 per cent a year. More than 40 per cent of the total deficit is accounted for by additional interest payments. If the aid were in gifts or low-rate loans, the cumulative deficit would fall to US $785 milliard, or 0·8 per cent of the cumulative GNP of the developed countries.

Kaldor's conclusion is that trade and aid are not alternatives and that the under-developed countries require massive support on both accounts over a long period. There is, of course, a clear distinction between the foreign exchange gap and the savings gap. Little and Clifford[3] point out that it is not generally true that the problem of under-developed countries is primarily one of foreign exchange. They suggest that most African countries export enough to pay for essential imports and that deficiency of savings is therefore the sole valid reason for giving aid. Even if this view may be too extreme, it supports a further major conclusion. However optimistic it is possible to be about fundamental reforms in the attitude of the aid-giving countries—and current indications are in the other direction—it is evident that the under-developed countries themselves will have to make a massive and sustained effort to raise their own rates of saving and thus finance a much larger proportion of the high rates of investment required for growth. The discussion here concentrates primarily on this problem.

It may be projected that the net domestic product in Africa could rise from US $32 milliard in 1960 to US $100 milliard in 1980 on the basis of a growth rate of 5·9 per cent.[4] This implies, of course, a considerable structural change. Thus the net domestic product for agriculture on the basis of these calculations would rise from US $11 to 30 milliard, and for industry from US $6·6 to 30 milliard, and that for other sectors from US $14 to 40 milliard.

The present annual level of capital investment in Africa is calculated at about US $4 to 4·5 milliard in 1960 prices. To achieve the growth rates indicated would mean raising capital formation to about US $20 milliard in 1980, i.e. from 14 per cent[5] of output in 1960 to 20 per cent in 1980. These figures are very large, but it should be borne in mind that the period of rapid development of the present advanced countries was not normally preceded by a considerable rise in the development of capital formation. On the contrary, acceleration of growth led to an increase in the level of capital formation. A further point is that the requirements of capital have been worked out on the basis of incremental capital–output ratios (ICOR's) assumed to be about 1·5 to 1 for agriculture, 2·5 to 1 for industry, and 4 to 1 for the rest of the economy. This gives an overall figure of 3 to 1, which obviously varies from country to country. Experience suggests that as the growth process gets under way, the ICOR falls partly because in the initial stages unused capacity and resources are drawn in, partly because of increased efficiency in the utilization of capital, and partly because tertiary industries use relatively little capital.[6] Furthermore, it is mainly in the industrial sector, and the trade related to it, that the incremental savings output ratio can be significantly higher than in agriculture, provided that trade unions confine their wage demands within increases of real labour productivity. Accordingly a serious attempt to increase capital formation requires increased industrial output (in the same way as the high rate of growth necessarily involves increased industrial output both absolutely and relatively). Thus a high marginal rate of savings can be assured if the share of industry, and particularly that of heavy industry, in national output is increased relative to that of other sectors.

The calculations above relate to global requirements of capital to achieve the rates of development suggested in the African economy as a whole. The rudimentary nature of many existing African development plans and the fact that most of them do not go beyond 1970 makes impossible an estimate of capital required to put into practice the intentions of the African governments themselves in the industrial sector. In any case, as they stand now the plans are conceived on a national basis and therefore seriously underestimate what could be done through co-operation. Rough estimates may be made of the capital requirements to carry out the industrial programmes sketched in Chapter IV. The estimates are derived from the ECA sources cited, but are not the ECA's. The order of magnitude of the total capital investment required for manufacturing industry in 1980 would be around US $4,000 million. This compares with a total capital formation estimated above to be feasible of US $20,000 million, i.e. 20 per cent. This is not only a much higher absolute figure than in any past year but also a significantly higher proportion of total formation. But it does not seem to be an inherently unreasonable one.

So far, requirements of capital have been examined. It is now proposed to examine prospects of meeting them to the greatest possible extent from domestic sources through higher rates of saving.

Data on current rates of domestic savings and investment are available only for some African countries and are set out in Table 5.

It is evident that the rates of investment which have prevailed in most countries in the past will have to be, and indeed in a number of cases are planned to be, substantially larger in the future. Leaving aside the special case of Gabon, only the United Arab Republic has an adequate rate of investment and it is the only country so far which is succeeding in transforming the structure of its economy. The second point is that rates of saving as a percentage of GDP are still lower, the exceptions being the mining economies of Gabon, Zambia, and the Democratic Republic of the

Congo. In such cases a substantial part of the savings accumulated flow out of the country. A further point to be made is that while a high average rate of saving is significant, high marginal rates are still more important, i.e. the ability to save a progressively higher

Table 5

CURRENT RATES OF DOMESTIC SAVINGS
AND INVESTMENT IN SELECTED AFRICAN
COUNTRIES IN 1961

| Country | GDP per caput US dollars | Rates of Savings % of GDP | Rates of Investment % of GDP | Savings per caput US dollars | Investment per caput US dollars |
|---|---|---|---|---|---|
| Ethiopia | 51 | 6·0 | 10·0 | 3·1 | 5·1 |
| Nigeria | 56 | 9·0 | 14·4 | 5·0 | 8·1 |
| Uganda | 60 | 7·0 | 11·1 | 4·2 | 6·7 |
| Tanganyika | 68 | 10·8 | 12·9 | 7·3 | 8·8 |
| Sudan | 72 | 9·0 | 14·2 | 6·5 | 10·2 |
| Mali | 79 | 4·1 | 7·0 | 3·2 | 5·5 |
| Congo (Dem. Rep.) | 100 | 14·0 | 15·2 | 14·0 | 15·2 |
| UAR | 156 | 10·0 | 24·0 | 15·6 | 37·4 |
| Tunisia | 157 | 8·0 | 17·9 | 12·6 | 28·1 |
| Morocco | 159 | 9·7 | 13·3 | 15·4 | 21·1 |
| Senegal | 165 | 8·3 | 15·0 | 13·7 | 24·7 |
| Cameroon | 168 | 7·0 | 10·0 | 11·8 | 16·8 |
| Fed. Rhodesia and Nyasaland | 175 | 23·9 | 16·0 | 41·8 | 28·0 |
| Ghana | 187 | 12·5 | 19·0 | 23·4 | 35·5 |
| Gabon | 203 | 32·2 | 32·3 | 65·4 | 65·6 |

*Source :* Data prepared by Belai Abbai, from ECA sources.

proportion of income as the latter rises. This has been demonstrated clearly in the case of North Africa.

It is of interest to examine in detail some of the assumptions of the latest development plans in Kenya, Tanzania, and Uganda.[7] Kenya is planning a GDP-volume growth rate of 7·5 per cent, an annual average contribution from domestic finance to the development budget of £1·2 million (less than in the recent past), and an annual average foreign contribution to the development budget of £12·2 million. Tanzania is planning a GDP-volume growth rate of 8·5 per cent, an annual average contribution to the development budget from domestic finance of £4·5 million, and an annual average foreign contribution of £15·9 million. Uganda until recently was planning a GDP-volume growth rate of 4 per cent, an annual average contribution to the development budget from domestic finance of £2·5 million, and £6·8 million from foreign finance. The share of gross investment in GDP is planned to be high, except originally in Uganda, respectively 23 per cent in Kenya, 26 per cent in Tanzania, and 14 per cent in Uganda (and as shown in Chapter II, the new plan is much more ambitious). Yet the respective assumptions concerning the share of foreign and domestic financial contributions to development both underestimate domestic possibilities and are unrealistic as to what can be obtained from abroad.

Clark analyses four constraints on larger development budgets in East Africa today: generalized saving, foreign exchange, government finance, and specialized manpower; and while recognizing that in absolute terms all four are constraints, he believes that the principal immediate one is government finance:[8] in other words, the chances of the government's commanding the financial means to make possible development of real resources for growth where available. He goes on to argue forcefully that East African governments ought to give greater emphasis to explicit plans for expanding the contribution of domestic finance to their development budgets, and shows how this in turn would facilitate the prospects of obtaining foreign aid where it is most needed.

It has been calculated[9] that to achieve a growth rate of GDP of 6 per cent in North Africa over the next twenty years, the increase in investment outlays could be reached if 50 per cent of the yearly per capita increment in national income were to be saved, in addition to the present 11·5 per cent of GDP. The marginal rate of saving (50 per cent) would be 4·4 per cent times higher than the average. This would raise savings by US $92 milliard over the twenty years, compared with an estimated total investment outlay required of US $93 milliard. This assumes also a 3·5 capital output ratio and ways and means of achieving external balance. This is a hypothetical but inherently plausible calculation which demonstrates the power of a reasonable domestic savings effort.

A further element in increasing domestic saving is related to the distribution of income, on which there is little precise information for Africa. Prebisch[10] has exposed the fallacy that 'only the capitalists save'. He has shown that 5 per cent of the population of Latin America account for 30 per cent of consumption and that the average consumption per household is fifteen times that of the lowest strata, which is 50 per cent of the population. Reduction from 15 to 1 to 11 to 1 would make possible an increase in the overall growth rate of from 1 to 3 per cent. Reduction to 9 to 1 (the US and Western European level) would make possible an increase in the growth rate of from 1 to 4 per cent.[11]

So far the impression is clear. There is much more scope for domestic saving than has hitherto been realized, and this despite the low per capita level of African incomes. There is a simple general principle which is not sufficiently understood. In the static economy of the textbook, it is argued that investment—which in a static situation is necessarily equal to saving—can increase only if consumption falls, and this is difficult when the economy is at or near a subsistence level. But investment generates income, which in turn makes possible increased saving. If the economy is growing fast enough, investment and consumption can both increase.

Public financing of economic development, including industry, must play a crucial role in Africa. This is not a doctrinal matter. The reason is simply that the alternatives available are inadequate and uncertain, and are bound to remain so for a long time to come. A related issue is self-financing of industrial expansion, particularly in the State and mixed sectors. None the less, despite the fact that progress is likely to be slow, there is much else to be done to promote domestic financing.

There are a number of ways in which domestic saving can be promoted, most of them obvious enough and yet insufficiently recognized in practice. Thus, small-scale saving can be mobilized in a variety of different ways. Equally significant is the identification of opportunities for domestic investment in a small-scale enterprise, this in turn promoting saving. Perhaps still more important is the need to attract small-scale investment into industry rather than land, or construction unrelated to either industry or agriculture. Diversion of savings into non-productive investment is notoriously a major vice in under-developed countries.

There is a need for institutions to mobilize domestic saving for local investments such as co-operative banks, unit trusts, and life insurance organizations. The industrial development bank is gradually gaining ground but has still a long way to go in most African countries, and here the International Bank can help, through both its International Development Association and its International Finance Corporation. Within the same context, domestic institutions for industrial promotion, to be examined in a later chapter, can also play a part in assisting small-scale industrialists to obtain capital equipment, loans at reasonable interest rates, and foreign exchange for imported raw materials and equipment; an example is the recently established organization in Gabon known as Promogabon, whose function is to promote small industry.

The industrial development corporation is more than a means of financing industry and is generally concerned with the development of the State or mixed sector. African experience of this device has not so far been particularly encouraging but there is an important exception, the Uganda Development Corporation.[12]

There remains to be considered another important instrument, fiscal policy, as a means of generating savings for all forms of development and thus also for industry. It is common knowledge that there is scope for better taxation systems in most African countries, in the double sense of the range of taxation and efficiency of collection. Some countries have made marked efforts, such as the UAR and Guinea, but they are the exception rather than the rule. According to an ECA Seminar, there is scope for more progressive taxation of personal incomes and for reaching farther down into the income-earning population.[13] The efficiency of taxation of business incomes can be greatly improved through better and more honest accounting and record-keeping. Looking to the future, and since the problem is as much one of administration and collection as the devising of effective systems, there is a need to break down the traditional dichotomy between taxation departments, the Treasury and the National Planning Authority. There is also scope for the devising of new taxes on internal production and expenditure, on land, property, wealth, and capital gains. The Seminar[13] also made an important recommendation for the establishment of an African Fiscal Programme along lines similar to that in Latin America.

Enough has been said to show not only the importance but also the essentially unexploited possibilities of domestic saving. Furthermore, a better domestic performance is one of the keys to attracting more foreign aid. There has been much debate recently in both official and academic circles on the future of foreign aid. At one extreme are the implications, sharply brought out by Kaldor, of the UN calculations. These are broadly accepted by Dudley Seers who has put forward a most comprehensive and ultimately logical scheme for a total reform of the aid process; in effect, he has proposed the evolution of a system of international taxation leading to automatic availability of sufficient quantities of aid on a continuing basis.[14] At the other end of the scale are some professional economists who seem to have persuaded themselves that to give aid at all is likely to do more harm than good. It can be shown that, although there has been little waste in foreign multilateral aid, there has been much waste in bilateral aid, both through the largely political predilections of the donors, and the practices of the governments in developing countries, not least in Africa. Furthermore, as has been shown, there is undoubtedly scope and need for a much greater effort on the part of the African governments themselves to raise the rate of productive investment and take steps to increase sharply domestic saving. None the less, large-scale and continuing foreign aid is necessary in a number of African countries, perhaps for the remainder of this century. On moral and ultimately on economic grounds, the case for multilateralized ways of aid as soon as possible is a strong one, and the proposals put forward by Dudley Seers, or some variants thereof, are surely the target to be worked for since they are likely in the long run to prove both efficient and just. Furthermore, they recognize that aid is not charity and that developing countries should be free to dispose largely at their own free will of whatever share of aid they may obtain. Realistically, however, bilateral aid in some form or another is bound to continue for some time.

The next step, therefore, is to restate briefly and perhaps somewhat dogmatically a series of propositions for improving the process of aid-giving.[15] The adoption of these would mean a great advance not only in itself but also as a step towards the ultimate multilateralization of aid.

1. It is becoming increasingly clear that aid should be given as far as possible on a national development plan basis, rather

than on a project basis, even though where countries are small and have no proper development plans it would be unrealistic to expect aid on a project basis to be discontinued at an early date.[16]

2. Aid should be calculated on the basis of total cost including domestic costs, less the possible domestic contribution.

3. Although from the point of view of the donor with balance of payments difficulties, tied aid is understandable, it is desirable that every effort should be made to move away from it on an agreed basis among the donor countries as quickly as possible.

4. The massive and growing burden of debt repayment demonstrates the importance of lengthening grace periods before repayment starts, of lengthening the period of the loan, and of low rates of interest. The worst type of loan is the suppliers' credit, which is bad in two senses: first, the period of repayment is short and the rate of interest high; secondly, it is frequently a device for foisting on developing countries high-priced machinery, with sometimes little relevance to well-considered and viable development projects. Almost all African countries have suffered in this way, at the hands of both Western and Eastern countries, and the large volume of short-term debt was a major factor in the recent change of government in Ghana.

5. For the same reasons underlying the last point, grants are preferable to loans and the proportion thereof should be greatly increased without imposing more than a nominal burden on the developed countries.

6. Despite all the difficulties of national budgeting and political pressures in the developed countries, it is of vital importance to the receivers of aid to know what they are likely to get over a reasonable period of time, say five years.

7. Although the main focus here has been on capital aid for industrial development, the small, and in general the poorest, countries in Africa can hardly begin to contemplate industrial development until their basic infrastructure has been greatly improved. There would therefore seem to be a case for grants on a massive scale, and indeed this is substantially what much of the current FED programme in Central and West Africa amounts to.

8. It has been clearly demonstrated that much industrial de-

velopment in Africa requires the grouping of countries and the sharing out of large-scale projects. This can be facilitated by appropriate measures on the part of the aid-giving and aid-receiving countries, both of whom will have to show more willingness to forget old colonial frontiers.

9. It has been current practice and it has been widely supported in academic circles that aid should be concentrated primarily on countries with the most absorptive capacity.[17] There is something to be said for giving more attention to exactly the opposite policy and concentrating a much larger slice of the soft loans and grants on the poorest countries, coupled, of course, with a determined effort to increase their absorptive capacity.

10. Much attention has been paid to the devising of suitable incentives as an inducement to foreign investors and almost all African countries have devised investment codes or laws offering tax holidays, favourable fiscal measures, protection against imports, provision for reasonable repatriation of profits, and assurances against nationalization without proper compensation.[18] Such measures are both reasonable and necessary but there is a danger of countries competing against one another to attract foreign investors and thus offer greater inducements than they need. A harmonized scheme of investment codes and incentives has been worked out by the group of countries which have joined the Treaty of UDEAC (the Republic of the Congo, Gabon, the Cameroon, Chad, and the Central African Republic), and there would seem to be scope for more sub-regional arrangements of this kind, and perhaps eventually an African charter. In so far as some discrimination is reasonable, it should be in favour of the weaker countries in a given grouping. Concerted action would also make it possible to ensure a higher degree of ploughing back of the profits of foreign investors for reinvestment in the country or sub-region concerned.

11. In recent years there has been an important development inspired in some degree by the Marshall Plan for Western Europe, by means of which the recipients of aid and the donors make joint arrangements for increasing the flow of aid, using it and sharing it out more effectively, e.g. the Colombo Plan and the Alliance for Progress. Similar arrangements for

Africa would seem to be desirable and are in fact being considered. A possible African council for economic co-operation has been proposed by the Executive Secretary of the ECA.[19]

In this context two other major points should be mentioned. One is the setting up of an African Development Bank under African direction, the capital of which is wholly subscribed by African governments. There is, however, provision for special loans or grants from outside Africa and the Bank is working closely with the International Bank, both in preparing projects and in its plans for financing. Furthermore, the agreement which led to the setting up of the African Development Bank gives priority to multinational projects. The second development, inspired by the success of the Consortia for India and Pakistan, is the establishment of consultative groups led by the International Bank and merging the efforts of a number of lenders or aid-givers. Nigeria, Tunisia, and East Africa are examples of receiving countries with consultative groups and there are others under consideration. There would seem to be scope for developing such consultative groups in relation to sub-regions or other multi-national partnerships.

Despite the need for reform and development in the aid-giving process, the fact remains that in recent years the amount of aid has not been increasing. For Africa, at least, this is attributed in considerable degree to the lack of sufficiently well-prepared projects, and there is evidence to support this contention. Even in Nigeria, which has generally been looked on with favour by international investors, the flow of external resources promised in support of the first development plan was seriously held up for the first two years owing to delays in project preparation. Yet Nigeria is better equipped for this task than most African countries. It was argued earlier in this chapter that too much attention is being focused on external rather than internal resources. Nevertheless, it is to be noted that the President of the International Bank has recently stated the following: 'A preliminary study made by the World Bank staff, utilizing available data and their own experienced judgement, suggests that the developing countries could put to constructive use, over the next five years, some US $3 to 4 billion more each year than is currently being made available to them.'[20]

A concluding note may therefore be the recognition that more foreign aid is needed in Africa and that there are a number of ways *on both sides* whereby the aid-giving process could be much improved. Yet the need for much greater efforts to mobilize domestic savings is apparent, and also the scope to do so.

There is one further important point. Developing countries, and most of all African countries, have to realize that whatever reforms may be introduced, the developed countries are bound to remain for a long time to come not wholly disinterested. They have shown themselves ready to promote the financing of infrastructure, human and physical. There are investors who are interested in promoting the creation of profitable new import substitution industries, generally on a national scale and concentrated to a considerable extent on consumer goods. There are fewer signs of a willingness to finance basic industry, intermediate and capital goods. This has to be recognized in a spirit of realism and can therefore be a guide to policy in the distribution of sources of finance. In other words, efforts can be made to attract external resources in directions of interest to the aid-givers, and in this context there are prospects of obtaining more in two key areas: human infrastructure and agriculture. The counterpart is for the African countries, by the grouping of their efforts, to finance basic industry largely from their own funds.

## NOTES AND REFERENCES TO CHAPTER VI

[1] *UN World Economic Survey 1962*, Part 1: 'The Developing Countries and World Trade', New York, 1963. There are widely diverging estimates of the magnitude of the foreign exchange gap, much lower estimates having been made, for example, by AID and B. Balassa. A reconciliation is attempted by F. G. Adams (*Alternative Projections of the Foreign Exchange Gap: A Reconciliation*, UNCTAD (document TD/B/C.3/30), Geneva, November 1966), and the lower estimates are shown to be largely the result of seemingly unrealistically low assumptions concerning import elasticities.

[2] N. Kaldor, 'International Trade and Economic Development', *Journal of Modern African Studies*, Vol. 2, No. 4 (Cambridge University Press, 1964). it should be stressed that this is Kaldor's hypothesis and that it is used here purely for illustrative purposes.

[3] I. M. D. Little and J. M. Clifford, *International Aid*, London, 1965, pp. 144–6.

[4] The calculations that follow are derived from an unpublished note by S. J. Patel.

[5] This may be on the low side since it is based on calculations which exclude mineral and settler countries where the rate of capital formation has been higher.

[6] At the present stage, an average gross capital output ratio for Africa may be nearer to 4 to 1 but there are good reasons to assume that it could be reduced.

[7] Paul Clark, 'Foreign Aid, Domestic Financing and the Development Plan', paper prepared for the University of East Africa Conference on Foreign Aid, Dar-es-Salaam, September 1964.

[8] P. Clark points out that there is considerable unused capacity, especially if continuous shifts were used, and other unused resources in East Africa which could rapidly be drawn in so that growth could be accelerated without any strain on the balance of payments or danger of inflation. Clearly, at a later stage, foreign exchange would be likely to be a major constraint, as is now true of Latin America. The fact that specialized manpower is not regarded as a constraint may seem curious, but, as Clark points out, while it is a matter of the highest priority to provide for improved education and training in development plans in the near future, there must necessarily be resort to specialized expatriate personnel which, if necessary, can be hired at a relatively small cost in relation to the total investment budget. It should be added that the bulk of this is obtainable in aid programmes and that the supply of technical advice and expert personnel is just as much capital aid as financial resources. It should also be added that, in the context of East Africa, government finance, i.e. recurrent expenditure for education and training, and development of skills are related.

[9] ECA, *Economic Survey of North Africa* (to be published).

[10] *Towards a Dynamic Development Policy for Latin America*, op. cit., pp. 31–32.

[11] Dudley Seers, in a paper entitled 'The Transmission of Inequality' contributed to a Seminar under the auspices of the Haile Selassie I Prize Trust Foundation, held in Addis Ababa in October 1966, has attempted a sketch of a general dynamic theory of the distribution of national income in poor countries. Although somewhat pessimistic in his conclusions as to what should be done, he brings out convincingly that a more equal distribution of income is a vital element in the development process, and although his reasoning is supported by social and political considerations, it is essentially economic in character.

[12] For an account of the experience of this Corporation, see *Financing of Industrial Development, with Particular Reference to Africa*, by Sir James Simpson, former Managing Director, contributed to the Symposium on Industrial Development in Africa (document CID/SYMP/B/11), Cairo, January–February 1966.

[13] The general considerations on taxation set out here are derived from the report of the Advanced Seminar on Current Problems and Training Needs in Taxation Administration, held in Addis Ababa in December 1965 (document E/CN. 14/FISC/1).

[14] Dudley Seers, 'International Aid, the Next Steps', *Journal of Modern African Studies*, Vol. 2, No. 4 (Cambridge University Press, 1964).

[15] Some of these are derived from Goran Ohlin, *Re-appraisals on Foreign Aid Policies*, OECD Development Centre, Paris, December 1964. This study examines the whole problem, with as its starting-point three recent national re-appraisals of foreign aid: the Clay Report, published in the United States; the Jeanneney Report, published in France; and a British White Paper on Aid to Developing Countries. G. Ohlin includes an extensive bibliography of recent contributions on the discussion of foreign aid.

[16] It is encouraging to note the elements of a change in policy in relation to Nigeria, where the International Bank and the Consultative Group have now agreed to provide programme support (see 'Backing Nigeria's Future', *West Africa*, No. 2542, 19 February 1966).

[17] Lewis has recently lent the weight of his authority to the idea that aid must not only be better used but therefore also more closely controlled by the donor countries (A. Lewis, *A Review of Economic Development*, op. cit.).

[18] For a summary of measures taken in Africa, see *Investment Laws and Regulations*, United Nations (Sales No. 65. II. K.3), New York, 1965. It should be noted that the precise measures are subject to fairly rapid change.

[19] This scheme involves an African Council at ministerial level, built-in procedures for regular consultations with donor countries, and a small permanent secretariat. It has been for some time under consideration by African governments, but decisions have not yet crystallized. On the other hand, the idea may prove to have been given further impetus by an ECA Resolution adopted at its eighth session held in Lagos in February 1967, largely inspired by a major speech by Mr. Tom Mboya which in effect again calls for an African 'Marshall Plan' (see E/CN. 14/393, resolution 169 (VIII) ).

[20] George D. Woods, 'The Development Decade in the Balance', *Foreign Affairs*, January 1966, p. 214.

K

# CHAPTER VII

# THE PREREQUISITES OF INDUSTRIAL DEVELOPMENT

So far, the place of industry in development has been examined, as well as the present pattern of industry in Africa and the prospects for industrial growth. The particular importance of the grouping of countries has been brought out and also the need for domestic capital formation. Agreement around these issues is beginning to crystallize. Yet the crucial steps remain to be considered: the prerequisites of industrial development (the subject of this chapter) and, still more important, the agents of industrialization, which are examined in the next.[1]

The prerequisites of industrial development considered here are science and technology and the application thereof, education, manpower planning, the discovery of natural resources, energy, and transport. This is evidently a wide field which cannot be discussed here in detail. An attempt is made to show the relationship of these problems to industrialization.

## SCIENCE AND TECHNOLOGY

Much of the discussion about science and under-developed countries has been bedevilled by the somewhat abstract conflict between pure and applied research, and in this context the United Nations Conference on the Application of Science and Technology for the Benefit of Less Developed Areas, held in Geneva in 1963, was not particularly illuminating. No one with any acquaintance with the progress of pure science, particularly in this century, can have the slightest doubt of the value of fundamental scientific development; from this it follows that developing countries cannot wholly disinterest themselves from it even today. Yet there have to be priorities, and in Africa, at least, the main emphasis at present must be on applied research oriented towards the solution of practical problems. The experience of Japan is significant. In the first stage, efforts were concentrated almost wholly on the transfer of technology from more developed countries, so much so that the Japanese acquired an unenviable, or perhaps in retrospect an enviable, record for copying other countries. From this they began to adapt the technology of others to their own needs. They then moved towards the final stage, the carrying out of their own fundamental research. This was paralleled in industry by the same three stages, the faithful copying of what was already established, adaptation of designs to their own needs, and then initiation of their own industrial designing. No comment is required on their success at this final stage in, for example, electronics and transport equipment. The USSR has been passing through similar phases. In Africa the UAR has also been successful in acquiring technology and industrial designs from other countries and is only now beginning to train its own industrial designers. It is far ahead of all other African countries in this respect.

The conclusion is a straightforward one, and it falls into three parts. First, mechanisms for the transfer of industrial technology; secondly, the commissioning of applied research on behalf of Africa in the developed countries wherever the efforts involved are complicated and expensive; and thirdly, arrangements within Africa for the carrying out of applied research, including the adaptation of existing technology to suit African conditions. Such conclusions may appear simple and evident but there is much to be done to make them effective in practice. The transfer of technology is complicated by awkward problems of property rights in know-how and patents. Education and training, so that Africans can acquire the necessary knowledge and apply it, are also essential. Little has been done so far by the developed countries to organize research, on however modest a scale, on behalf of African countries. It is true that much research on African problems is carried out, particularly in England and France, but it is primarily directed to the solution of problems of interest to commercial bodies in these countries: for example, corrosion of metals and the growing and processing of primary products such as edible oils, coffee, and cocoa. In the third area, applied research in Africa, a start has hardly been made. It has been estimated by UNESCO that of 3,428 research workers in Africa in 1963 only 71 were engaged on industrial research.

The approach, given the size and financial resources of most

African countries, has to be by grouping of efforts, and to be
linked organically with national arrangements for industrial promotion, a subject discussed in the next chapter. The principal
priorities in the industrial field are apparent: food processing,
particularly for domestic or African markets, including fish processing, production of animal feeding stuffs, production of animal
vaccines, and production of bread flour—with ingredients of African origin, e.g. groundnut and cotton-seed oil and fish flour;[2]
timber manufactures, both for export and domestic markets; transformation of metals, mainly for African markets but also for export,
and especially, at the present stage, copper and aluminium, with
research into the adaptation of processes with a view to accelerat-
ing or starting production of metal products of all kinds, particularly agricultural tools, mechanical and electrical engineering
products, and transport equipment.[3] In Chapter I there was some
discussion of the choice of technology, and reference to some of the
current confusions or illusions. None the less, it is evident that there
is much scope for research within Africa on the devising or adapting of suitable processes. Furthermore, the guiding principle should
be to look for simple and relatively inexpensive research whenever
possible, in which Africans from the start play a real part in the
research process.[4]

Steps are now being taken to establish on a group basis applied
research centres in Africa. The four Maghreb countries have jointly obtained from the UNDP support for a centre for industrial
studies, to be located in Tripoli. Its major task will be to undertake
studies of the industrial development of an area or sector of the
economy of the four countries, or any study of industrial projects
which it may be requested to carry out in the joint interest of two
or more countries. The centre will work partly with personnel from
national development agencies. It will promote industrial standardization on a co-ordinated basis. It will set up a documentation
service. Two points should be emphasized: the role of the centre in
promoting industrial co-ordination and the deliberate links to be
forged with national centres. An alternative approach has been
adopted in East Africa, consisting of an administrative council for
the whole sub-region, together with a deliberately worked out
scheme for a division of labour in industrial research among the
different countries, each one specializing and servicing the others
in that field.

## EDUCATION

Education is obviously a prerequisite to any kind of development in the world today, particularly in industry. In recent years there has been wider recognition of the economics of human resources. This has been due in no small measure to Harbison, with his path-breaking study of Nigerian requirements and the part he played in stimulating two major UNESCO conferences.[5] In this brief account of the main features of the African educational system at present and the tasks ahead, free use has been made not only of the reports of the UNESCO conferences but also more recent works by Harbison and his colleagues.[6]

In assessing the educational progress of a country, two different factors have to be considered: the stock of educated personnel at different levels and the additions or means of addition to this stock. More precisely, this involves numbers enrolled at the first, second, and third levels of education, qualified teachers, and respective percentage enrolment in science and technology faculties and in the humanities, fine arts, and law. It also involves consideration of the numbers being trained to become high-level manpower, distinguishing the proportions among five categories: entrepreneurial, managerial, and administrative in both the public and private sectors; professional, particularly scientists, engineers, and agronomists; qualified teachers; sub-professional and technical personnel down to the top levels of skilled craftsmen; and leaders in politics, law, and the armed forces.

Harbison and Myers have worked out a composite index using a system of weighting of the different elements in the educational system referred to in the last paragraph, and by dividing countries into four levels. Most African countries fall into level one, with a GDP per capita, measured in US dollars, of less than 100. In the second category, with a GDP up to 200, there are a few more African countries such as Tunisia and Ghana, and only one, the UAR, at the third level. For purposes of comparison the average GDP in the fourth category is US $1,100.

The differences among the four levels can now be illustrated. Teachers at the first and second levels of education per 10,000 of the population are, respectively, 17, 38, 33, and 80. Scientists and engineers per 10,000 of the population are respectively 0·6, 3, 25, and 42. For the first level enrolment ratios the differences are less marked, from 22 to 73. For the second level the respective ratios are 2·7, 12, 27, and 59. For the third level they are 0·5, 1·6, 5, and 11.

The differences between the respective percentages enrolled in scientific and technical faculties and in the humanities, fine arts, and law faculties are much less marked, ranging from 24 to 28 and 34 to 32 respectively.

Harbison and Myers have also worked out a ranking of countries by composite indexes which is not very different from what might be expected, starting with:

| | |
|---|---|
| 0·3 in Niger | 5·0 in Nigeria |
| 1·6 in Somalia | 5·5 in Senegal |
| 2·6 in the Ivory Coast | 7·5 in the Sudan |
| 3·6 in the Democratic | 15·2 in Tunisia |
| Republic of the Congo | 23·2 in Ghana |
| 4·7 in Kenya | 40·1 in Egypt |

(These are, of course, illustrative and not complete.) As a basis for comparison, the index for the United Kingdom is 121·6, and for the United States 261·3.

These figures speak for themselves and some light on the roots of the problem is thrown by Berg.[7] It is pointed out that in three key countries in former French West Africa the main line of French thinking in the early fifties was to hold the aggregate investment in education constant or even to reduce it, to put greater emphasis on technical education, and also to increase the proportion of education investments in primary schools.

The indispensable instrument for the creation of high-level manpower, a predominant secondary school base, was explicitly rejected; also secondary school enrolments rose less in French-speaking West Africa during the crucial years of the late fifties than in many other African areas.[8]

The comparative figures from 1954 to 1957 were:

| | per cent |
|---|---|
| Nigeria | 77 |
| Uganda | 117 |
| Northern Rhodesia | 114 |
| Belgian Congo | 26 |
| French West Africa | 23 |

In 1956 some twenty-four Africans were enjoying a higher level of education in the whole of French West Africa, most of them assistant teachers, midwives, pharmacists, and veterinarians.

Berg arrives at four main conclusions. First, the primary school must be transformed from a producer of semi-illiterates divorced from their milieu into an instrument of mass education, particularly rural education. Secondly, upper-level secondary education must be increased far beyond its present capacity. As he says: 'It is grotesque and wasteful beyond calculation to have over-capacity at the University level and a void in higher-level manpower occupations while large numbers of primary school and junior secondary school graduates (whose costly education has prepared them for little except further education) find no place in upper secondary classes.'[9] Thirdly, there is a need for innovation in education to lighten the deadening of rote learning and the tyranny of examinations. Fourthly, given high drop-out rates and other cost-raising factors, he suggests that before increasing resources are devoted to education, the efficiency of existing systems, including trade and vocational schools, should be given first priority.

Before attempting to draw some conclusions on educational policies from the point of view of industrial development it is of interest to consider the contrast between East Africa, which, as has been shown, is better off than ex-French West Africa (and *a fortiori* Central Africa), but less well placed than Nigeria and Ghana, and selected Asian countries. Hunter has made these comparisons.[10] He characterizes the East African situation from the point of view of education as follows: some preparatory training for independence, some degree of Africanization of the civil service, a very small but high-quality system of higher education, concentration of such high-level African manpower as was available in government service, a reasonably well-developed system of agricultural extension, some degree of large-scale agriculture (admittedly in expatriate hands), and a sizeable commercial sector, mainly in Asian hands. In contrast, taking Burma and Indonesia as examples (as he points out, Malaysia is more similar to East Africa), there was no serious administrative or managerial preparation before independence, a shaky central administration, an extensive university system of doubtful quality based on rapidly expanded secondary schools, a surplus of educated manpower in many fields, especially in Burma, poorly developed agricultural services, and a high degree of nationalization, linked with shortage of managerial skill and discouragement of foreign enterprise. The conclusions drawn, which apply to the Far East but could well apply also to East Africa if preventive steps are not taken in time, are as follows: a swollen and untrained civil service, particularly in the middle and lower ranks; a too rapidly expanded university system and secondary school system characterized by excessive drop-outs and poor teaching; neglect of agricultural extension; and a shortage of managerial skill, coupled with a surplus of high-level manpower in other disciplines seeking suitable employment.

Turning back to Africa, some conclusions for the strategy of educational advance can be drawn. Perhaps too high a proportion of educated high-level manpower is employed in government service. The time is not far off even in ex-French territories when all the top ministerial and high-level administrative posts will be in the hands of Africans. Yet the strategic technical positions in the public service, in private industry and commerce, and even in higher education are still held by non-indigenous personnel. The same is true of agriculture, at least as far as exported produce is concerned. Primary education has been over-stressed, including the goal of universal literacy. Secondary education, particularly in the upper levels, is being underestimated. The teaching profession, again primarily at the secondary level, is being neglected. This is partly a result of too low salary scales, although in the longer run these have to be set at a lower level than those of expatriates. Much more stress has to be laid on technological subjects, including as a background mathematics and general science. The proportion of students enrolled in scientific and technological subjects, including medicine and agriculture, should reach at least 60 per cent by 1980. Within this general area of scientific and technological subjects perhaps some 40 per cent should be expected to take a full degree course and the rest be trained at the sub-professional and technical level. Some African students have to be sent abroad for higher education, but the present system is an indiscriminate one and needs to be controlled much more severely by governments, both in respect of the courses taken and the subsequent employment of those trained.

W. C. Cash has drawn attention to the possibility that high-level manpower planning in Africa can be a cause of over-investment in education. He suggests that there are four key issues: enlargement of the highly educated élite, research, the need to look throughout the educational system for potential managers or entrepreneurs, and teacher-training.[11] The implications as to what cannot be done, given scarcity of resources, are evident.[12]

The main lines of policy for education in Africa as a factor in economic development are authoritatively summarized by an African Working Party (the ECA's Working Party on Manpower and Training) in the following words:

1. Considering that only a small proportion of those passing through primary education is likely to proceed to higher levels of education or training, the Working Party recommends that the curricula in primary education should be re-examined in the light of manpower needs and with a view to adjusting the aspirations of school-leavers to realistic employment opportunities in the economy. To this end Governments should also consider appropriate modifications in the curricula of teacher-training institutions.

2. Although the desirability of achieving universal, free primary education is recognized, it is recommended, in view of the experience in some of the African countries, that Governments should not feel impelled to achieve this goal too rapidly at the expense of other national priorities of economic development.

3. It should be recognized that a high proportion of those actually producing goods and services in Africa receive little or no formal education. It is therefore recommended that Governments should give more attention to the need for raising their productivity through some form of training. The role of adult education and youth services should be recognized in such matters.

4. Taking into consideration the bottleneck created by shortage of middle-level manpower in most African countries, resulting from insufficient numbers of secondary school-leavers with a science, technical and practical background, it is recommended that Governments should take positive action to increase the number of secondary school students with science and technical background.

5. The relative proportions of students in the humanities on the one hand, and in science and technology on the other, are inconsistent with Africa's requirements from the point of view of economic development. It is therefore recommended that Governments should take steps to ensure that enrolment in various faculties of universities reflects the manpower needs in the African region.

6. In order that the optimum utilization of all available national resources may be directed towards meeting the manpower requirements of the economy, it is recommended that Governments should take steps

to ensure that opportunities for education and training abroad are utilized only as a supplement to local facilities.[13]

Thus far we have outlined the almost universal problems in Africa of the educational system, with particular reference to preparation for industrialization. The next chapter will examine training. A final word may be said about the scope for African co-operation. Universities are proliferating in Africa and even where there has been a degree of unification, as in East Africa, it is tending to break up, with duplication and waste of human and financial resources. The tendency should be the other way and a lead has recently been given by President Johnson in the reformulation of American aid policy in relation to Africa, with more emphasis on the regional approach.[14] There is much to be said for a deliberate effort on the part of African universities to specialize, thus economizing on scarce resources and making possible a deepening of the content of courses given. Possible examples may be given. It would be reasonable to specialize in engineering technology in Lagos, Cairo, Nairobi, and Dakar; chemical technology and petroleum engineering could be developed in the North African Universities; there could be specialization in the social sciences, and particularly economics, which is of vital importance for industrial development, in Lovanium and Makerere; the University of Senegal might specialize in the whole field of multi-purpose river development; the new University of Zambia could specialize in mining. These are simply examples of a profitable way forward in the development of higher education in Africa.

## MANPOWER PLANNING

An effective manpower plan must stretch back and have its influence on the shape of the education system, just as it looks forward to the construction of detailed training programmes. Few African countries have carried out reasonably adequate manpower surveys, the main exceptions being the UAR, Tunisia, Nigeria, Kenya, Rhodesia, Ghana, and the Ivory Coast.[15] The need for comprehensive manpower surveys in every African country is surely evident: to identify the critical shortages of skilled manpower in each major sector of the economy, to identify actual or potential surpluses and why they have arisen, and to set out future targets in some detail. The problem is both quantitative and qualitative, and the absence of adequate statistics in many countries is no reason for doing nothing. The translation of a manpower plan into training requirements will be considered in the next chapter and illustrative figures will be given for selected countries. The key to the solution is the recognition of the problem and the establishment of manpower planning in each country, linked with the national planning machinery. Few African plans have much to say about manpower, or the proper liaison with educational planning, looking backwards, and effective liaison, looking forwards, with machinery for the establishment and carrying out of detailed training programmes. African countries are not wholly unaware of the need for such machinery. What is lacking are trained specialists in manpower planning.

## THE DISCOVERY OF NATURAL RESOURCES

It is a commonplace that Africa is well endowed with most natural resources, that they are insufficiently exploited, and that too little is known of them. Because of lack of knowledge, particularly of the resources of the smaller and poorer countries, it is sometimes argued that it is premature to envisage sub-regional arrangements for industrial development, since any agreements entered into might be unfair to some countries. The contrary approach is adopted here. Sufficient is already known for vast schemes of industrial development, as has been brought out in Chapter IV. The right way is to concentrate efforts on the weaker countries and here much can be expected from the United Nations family and the bilateral donor countries, through grants and technical assistance. Furthermore, it is in the interest of the more prosperous African countries to help their weaker brothers in this respect if they want them to take part in effective and durable sub-regional economic groupings. It was brought out in Chapter V to what degree efforts towards integration have so far been weakened through neglect of the poorer countries. In practice, this means in the first instance intensified mineral surveys in such countries as Tanzania, Malawi, the Central African Republic, Chad, Niger, Upper Volta, Mali, and Mauritania. These efforts may be assisted by suitable research institutes set up on a co-operative basis covering water, agricultural, and mineral resources. There are tentative plans for two such institutes, one serving East Africa and the other the whole Sahil–Sudan Zone.[16]

## ENERGY[17]

Africa is rich in water-power and in some areas also in oil and natural gas. Its coal resources are limited. In the case of oil, the principal and of course very extensive resources are to be found in North Africa, Nigeria, and Gabon, but there is intensive prospection in progress in several other countries.

Consumption of primary energy is low. Measured in coal equivalent it is 300 kg. per capita in the UAR, and about 50 to 70 kg. per capita in most of Africa south of the Sahara, in some countries even lower. For the purposes of comparison, it is 2,500 kg. in South Africa. These figures are essentially a measure of industrial development.

It has been found that in industrialized countries energy consumption grows on the average at 7·3 per cent a year, corresponding to a doubling in ten years. In developing countries the rate is twice as high, but there are marked differences among regions. Thus during the fifties the rate of growth was 18 per cent in the Far East, 15 per cent in Latin America, and only 9 per cent in Africa. Although this study is not concerned with energy as such, it is appropriate, given the importance of industrialization as a factor governing energy consumption and also, as is evident, the great need for abundant and cheap energy as a pre-condition of industrial development, to set out the main factors in an energy investment policy.

The investment cost per ton of primary energy, measured in US dollars, is as follows:

| | |
|---|---|
| Lignite | 10–17 |
| Coal | 20–35 |
| Crude oil | 40–60 |
| Natural gas | 40–60 |

The investment per ton in coal equivalent for electric energy is as follows:

| | |
|---|---|
| Thermal | 94 |
| Nuclear | 100–140 |
| Hydroelectric | 263–368 |

Finally, the ranking order of the total production cost of different types of energy is measured by the following figures:

| | |
|---|---|
| Hydroelectric power | 4·6–5·7 |
| Natural gas | 5·0–13·2 |
| Coal | 9·4–14·7 |
| Crude oil | 12·8 |
| Thermoelectric | 14·0 |

The favourable position of hydroelectric power when it is abundant is evident and the advantages may be still greater, since large-scale power development schemes in Africa are normally associated with multi-purpose development: irrigation, navigation, and so forth.

The number of large-scale hydroelectric schemes installed, in the course of installation, or envisaged, is thus easily explained. The principal examples are the Aswan Dam (ultimate capacity, 2,100 MW), the Volta River in Ghana (ultimate capacity 760 MW), the Kainji Dam in Nigeria (initially 320 MW and ultimately 960 MW), the Kariba Dam in Rhodesia (ultimate capacity 1,500 MW), Inga in the Democratic Republic of the Congo (first stage, 200 MW, and ultimate capacity 30,000 MW), Kouilou in the Republic of the Congo (1,100 MW), Konkoure in Guinea (360 MW), and Gouina in Mali.

The size of most of these schemes is such that to realize their full potential they need outlets in neighbouring countries. In particular some of them can only be realized if there are set up energy intensive industries.

Existing inter-connexions among African countries are as follows:

Democratic Republic of the Congo–Zambia
Democratic Republic of the Congo–Republic of the Congo
Zambia–Rhodesia
Rhodesia–Mozambique–South Africa
Kenya–Uganda

Among possibilities which are either under discussion or feasible are the following:

1. Electric power inter-connexion in three stages, the first step being the supply from Akosombo of the Ivory Coast, Togo,

Dahomey, and Ghana; the second stage the setting up of a joint arrangement between Dahomey and Togo based on the harnessing of the Mono River and the development of the Kossou project in the Ivory Coast, and the third stage a link with the Nigerian system.[18]

2. The harnessing of the Senegal River at Gouina to serve Mali, Senegal, and Mauritania.

3. The harnessing of the Konkoure to serve Guinea and Mali.

4. The supply of electric power from Algeria, on the basis of natural gas, to Morocco and Tunisia. It is estimated that this would save at least US $30 million in capital over the next few years and $1 million a year in current expenditure.[19]

Of the other major schemes, the Aswan Dam is a national multipurpose project. Kainji is a national project which will assure Nigerian supplies for the next decade. The Akosombo (Volta River) is being set up and Konkoure is envisaged, primarily on the basis of aluminium, but there would be much advantage in interconnexions as indicated. The extension of Kariba must now be in doubt in the light of political changes. Inga can be built up by stages and the present thinking is primarily in terms of national industrial development. There would, however, be economic advantage in continuing development to a further stage to supply part of the growing needs of the Republic of the Congo. Kouilou has to be built up in one stage and its future depends therefore on establishing large-scale production for export of aluminium and ferro-alloys. The electro-metallurgical complex has to be carried out as one project.

Oil refineries have been or are being established in many African countries, mainly at coastal sites. There is one example of a co-operative project: the five countries of the UDEAC have agreed to establish jointly a refinery at Port Gentil in Gabon to serve the whole area. It might be worth examining the possibility of piping oil from Nigeria to Fort Lamy and setting up a refinery there to serve a group of hinterland countries: Chad, the Central African Republic, north Cameroon, northern Nigeria, Niger. A second refinery might be established in Mali to serve the remainder of the energy-deprived hinterland of West Africa. This would be the more possible if, as is to be hoped, extensive oil is discovered in Mali.

Some solution has to be found for countries in this category, at present dependent on oil generally moved enormous distances on inadequate roads and on small-scale diesel stations, thus leading to very high costs. The harnessing of African hydro-power resources, particularly within the framework of inter-country connexions, is only one aspect of the solution to Africa's energy problem. The other is much more intensive effort to assist countries poor in energy resources. Apart from the suggestions already made, more can be done to establish small-scale hydro-power stations and to make use of solid fuel resources such as lignite. Lack of cheap energy need not be an obstacle to the industrialization of Africa, but the fact remains that in many countries it still is.

## TRANSPORT[20]

Industry and transport are frequently connected in a vicious circle. Industrialization is hampered by lack of transport. Transport investment cannot be justified economically without more trade, particularly intra-African trade, which in turn depends on industrial development. The problem, a vital one for industry, is how to break out of this circle.

It is familiar that the main transport routes in Africa from the coast to the interior are a means of evacuating agricultural produce and minerals for export, and of supplying the interior with imported goods. The transport system of Africa can be divided into three main categories: what are known as the penetration routes already referred to, the means of integration, and the national systems, made up primarily of feeder roads.

There are six principal penetration routes in Africa south of the Sahara.[21]

1. The Sudanese railway, running from Port Sudan to Nyala and Wau and Juba.
2. The Kenya–Uganda railway running from Mombasa through Nairobi to Tororo, with a branch northwards to Gulu and beyond and a branch westwards to Kasese.
3. The Tanzanian railway running from Dar-es-Salaam to Kigoma, with a branch northwards to Mwanza and another southwards in the direction of Zambia.

# MAP 2

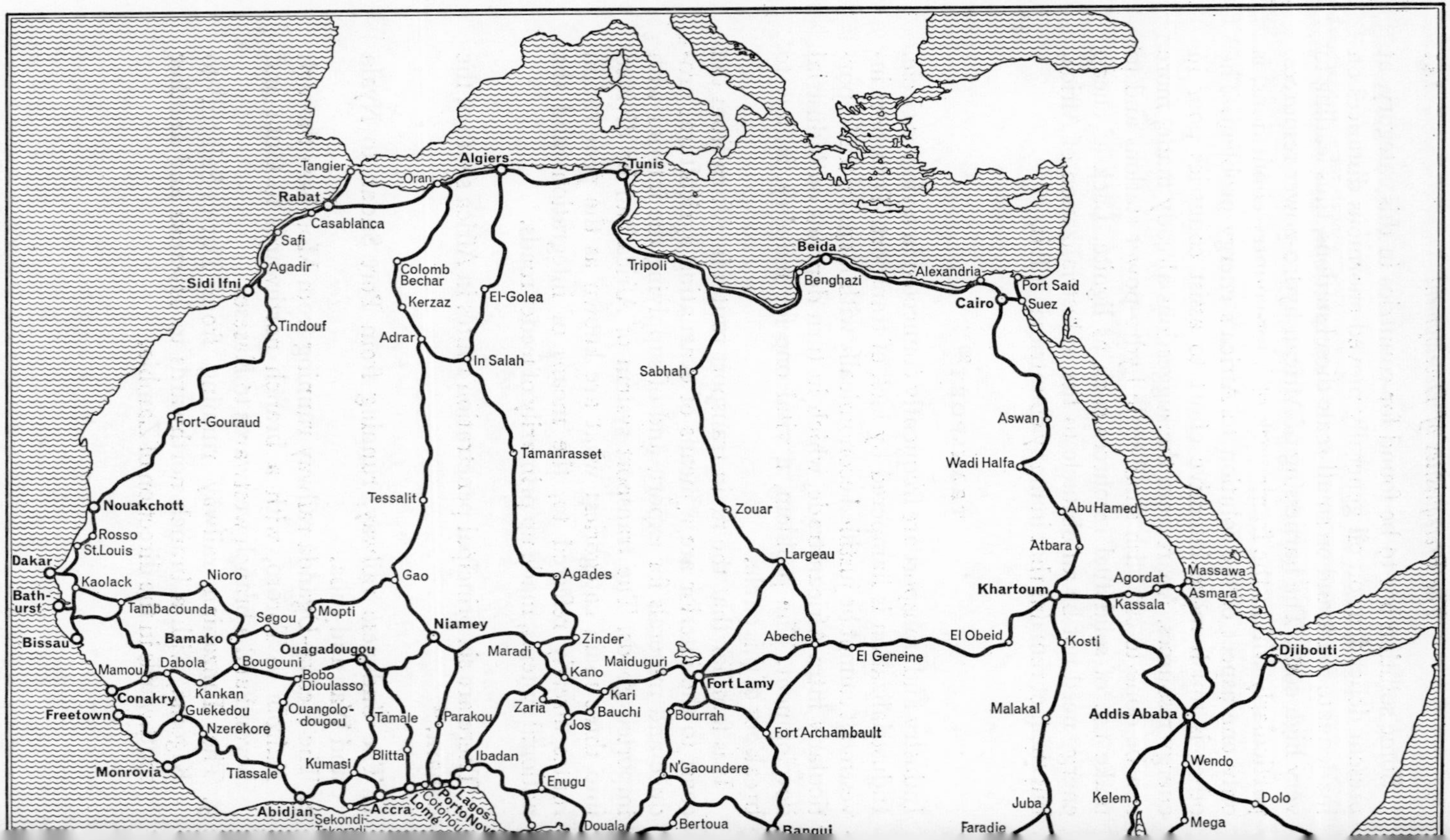
Tangier
Algiers
Tunis
Oran
Rabat
Casablanca
Safi
Agadir
Sidi Ifni
Tindouf
Colomb Bechar
Kerzaz
El-Golea
Adrar
In Salah
Tripoli
Beida
Benghazi
Alexandria
Port Said
Cairo
Suez
Sabhah
Fort-Gouraud
Tamanrasset
Aswan
Wadi Halfa
Tessalit
Zouar
Abu Hamed
Nouakchott
Rosso
St.Louis
Dakar
Kaolack
Nioro
Gao
Agades
Largeau
Atbara
Bath-urst
Tambacounda
Segou
Mopti
Niamey
Zinder
Abeche
El Obeid
Khartoum
Agordat
Kassala
Massawa
Asmara
Bissau
Bamako
Ouagadougou
Maradi
Maiduguri
El Geneine
Kosti
Djibouti
Mamou
Dabola
Bougouni
Bobo Dioulasso
Kano
Fort Lamy
Conakry
Kankan
Kari
Freetown
Guekedou
Ouangolo-dougou
Tamale
Parakou
Zaria
Bauchi
Jos
Bourrah
Malakal
Addis Ababa
Nzerekore
Fort Archambault
Monrovia
Tiassale
Kumasi
Blitta
Ibadan
N'Gaoundere
Wendo
Enugu
Juba
Kelem
Dolo
Abidjan
Sekondi-Takoradi
Accra
Lomé
Cotonou
Porto Novo
Lagos
Douala
Bertoua
Bangui
Faradie
Mega

Routes in the Republic of South Africa are not shown

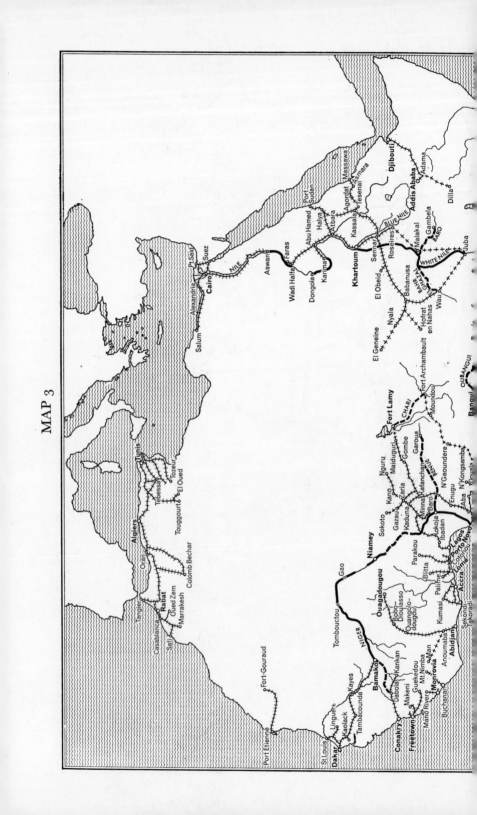

MAP 3

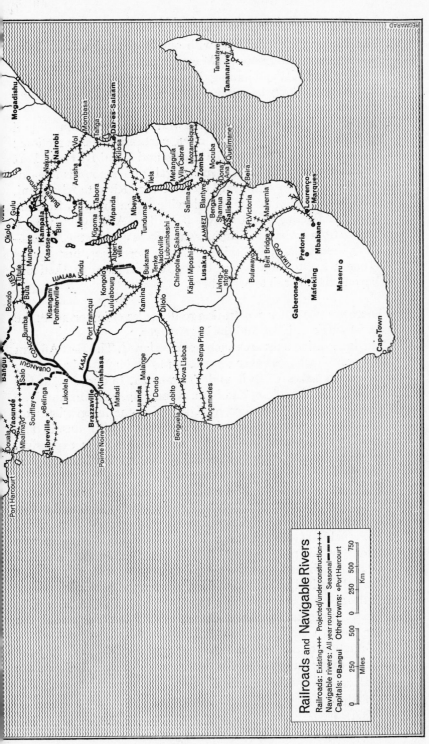

Routes in the Republic of South Africa and in South-West Africa are not shown

4. The Mozambique railway, with one line running from Beira and another from Lourenço Marques, converging at Somabula, crossing Zambia, and joining the Congo system.
5. The Angola–Congolese system starting from Lobito and joining up with the Congolese system at Tenke.
6. The Congolese system. This starts with the railway from Matadi to Kinshasa and is then part river, part rail, in three sections: the first is to the south by the Congo and Kasai Rivers to Port Francqui where the railway starts again; the second is towards the east and then southward by the Congo River to Kisangani, then a rail section to Ponthierville, then by the Lualaba River to Kindu, and then on by rail to Albertville, with a branch from Kabalo to Kamina which joins up with the Angola–Congolese system; the third is to the north-east, first by the Congo River to Bumba then by the Itimbiri River to Aketi and beyond that by rail to Mungbere.

There are two other penetration routes of lesser importance: the Dakar–Bamako railway and the Niger River.

The integration axes are much less developed. The East African railway and harbours cover from Ruvu to Kalembwani and ferry transport on Lakes Victoria and Tanganyika. In addition, as has been seen, the Congolese, Zambian, Rhodesian, and Mozambique rail systems are inter-connected. Otherwise, the integration axes consist almost entirely of roads of mediocre quality unsuited to modern traffic, where, as will be seen, transport is expensive. The exceptions are the international rivers, but for the most part these are navigable only part of the year.

The third main group, the national systems, need not be considered in detail here. Much is being done within national transport programmes, with significant aid from the World Bank, FAC (the French aid programme), FED (the European Economic Community aid programme), British aid programmes, and US AID. But much more remains to be done. From an economic point of view, the principal issue is to facilitate the commercialization of agriculture by making possible the collection of produce and its transport to the main arteries. On the other side of the medal, the feeder road system facilitates the distribution of industrial goods.

The nature of the African transport system explains vividly the obstacles to the integration of industrial programmes. Railways are characterized by high fixed charges. Subsequent costs in proportion to traffic are relatively low. Consequently, average costs decline steeply as traffic rises. In the nature of things this normally means bulky goods and long distances. As soon as a traffic density of 300,000 to 500,000 ton/kilometres (t/km.) is attained, the average cost is significantly lower than that of road transport. This makes it possible to practise a discriminatory tariff policy based on the nature of the goods transported and falling rapidly with distance. The Sudanese railways charge an average cost of US cents 1·5 per t/km. and this falls as low as 0·3 cents for class 17 traffic (fertilizers) for distances of the order of 2,500 km.

The cost of transport by inland waterways depends on the nature of the river, essentially the depth of water and the degree to which the river is navigable all the year round. The Congo and Kasai Rivers are the cheapest in Africa. A convoy of 2,000 tons on the Congo River costs 0·3 US cents t/km., including loading and unloading. On the other African rivers charges are significantly higher.

In the case of road transport tariffs are proportional to volume, since there are no fixed charges. If the volume of traffic to be carried increases, a proportional increase in the number of lorries is required. In Africa the average cost is of the order of US cents 4 to 5 t/km., rising sometimes to 6 and not falling below 3 save in exceptional cases in large towns or ports where full loads all the time and limited turn-round delays are feasible.

If these considerations as to the nature of the African transport system are now related to costs, and penetration routes compared with integration axes, it will be seen that the cost ratios are 1 to 3 or 4, and sometimes as much as 1 to 20. Thus it will be seen that fertilizers can be transported from Port Sudan to Juba, a distance of 2,800 km., at a cost of approximately US $8 per ton. If fertilizers were to be manufactured near Kampala (Uganda) and delivered to Juba, a distance of only 900 km., the cost of transport per ton would be about US $40. This is an extreme but not wholly untypical case and demonstrates clearly that without transport improvements of the right kind, sub-regionally co-ordinated industrial development in Africa is largely illusory. In this particular case it should be noted that the essence of the matter is quite simply transport. The hypothesis is that fertilizers could be manufactured near Kampala at a cost equal to the landed cost at Port Sudan of fertilizers manufactured abroad. This hypothesis, as has been shown in Chapter IV, is a realistic one. The point can be driven home by a further simple illustration. If the transport tariff is divided by 2, the geographical area is multiplied by 4 and the market also if the population is divided evenly; if the tariff is divided by 3, the market area is multiplied by 9. The tariff range is at least 1 to 12. Two conclusions can be drawn. One is that frequently, with existing transport networks, there is a natural protection against the products of both the outside world and the neighbour and hence an obstacle to collaboration with neighbours. The second is that the existence of a penetration route and the non-existence of a cheap integration route (as in the illustration given from the Uganda and the Sudan) is a severe obstacle to co-operation with neighbours owing to the overwhelming force of external competition in what would otherwise be a natural market area for a multinational plant.

The next step, therefore, is to examine in broad outline the shape of the transport development programmes in Africa, particularly from the point of view of improving the integration axes. The first point to be noted is that some of the recent major ventures or plans are concerned more to develop penetration routes. This is true, for example, of the Miferma railway in Mauritania, the Liberian railway system, and the projected Mekambo railway in Gabon, all concerned with the evacuation of iron ore. The Congo–Ocean railway, in the Republic of the Congo, is being improved with a view to export of potash. The main apparent justification for a railway link between the Trans-Cameroon and Bangui, in the Central African Republic, is for the export of timber. These schemes are not necessarily unjustified from an economic point of view but they demonstrate that so far thinking is changing slowly. The main lines of an improved integration system which might be justified in the next ten to fifteen years can be indicated briefly.

In West Africa there are three main links which are required and prima facie feasible:

1. A hinterland link from approximately Bamako (Mali) to approximately Kano (Nigeria) along the line of the Ghana–Upper Volta border. This might be either road or rail.
2. Improved coastal communications. On the face of it, the case is for improved coastal shipping facilities from Port Etienne

(Mauritania) to Abidjan (Ivory Coast). From Abidjan east-
ward the connexion might be by improved coastal shipping,
by rail, or by road. A rail link between Cotonou and Lagos
would also be significant in integrating the Lagos–Cotonou
port system.
3. Improved navigation facilities on the Niger River.

In Central Africa the connexions across the Democratic Republic of the Congo are reasonable. There is a strong prima facie
case for a bridge across the Congo River, thus linking up with the
Congo–Ocean railway and the port of Pointe Noire, which has
immense possibilities for development, and the eventual improvement of the evacuation system from Katanga and Zambia. Work
is proceeding to improve the road connexion between Libreville
(Gabon) and Yaounde (Cameroon), and between Yaounde and
Fort Lamy (Chad), partly by extension of the Trans-Cameroon
railway, on which work is already in hand, and partly by improved
road links farther north. The Governments of Chad and the Central African Republic have decided to share the cost of asphalting
the road between Fort Lamy and Bangui. As already noted, the
United Nations Special Fund is expected to start shortly a study
of transport links between the Cameroon and the Central African
Republic. The link between the Central African Republic and the
Democratic Republic of the Congo is now the Oubangui–Congo
waterway, the depth of which could be increased at relatively
little investment, thus facilitating a greater flow of traffic at
cheaper rates. To complete the integration of Central Africa, two
more links are required which have still to be seriously examined.
One is between the Cameroon and the Democratic Republic of the
Congo. Assuming that the Trans-Cameroon railway is eventually
extended to Bangui and that the navigability of the Sangha River
is improved, it would seem that this link could be provided at relatively modest cost through a branch southward from the Trans-
Cameroon to the point where the Sangha River becomes fully
navigable. Secondly, the full integration of Gabon within Central
Africa would seem to depend on an extension of the Mekambo
railway to link up with the Trans-Cameroon.
Before moving farther east, reference should be made to the
scope for closing the gap between the Nigerian railways at Maiduguri. The extension of this railway has been conceived within the

framework of an ambitious project to link up the Nigerian and Sudanese railway systems by crossing Chad. This project would seem to be one for the future, but the improvement of the road connexion between the Nigerian railhead and Fort Lamy would be a relatively inexpensive operation which might soon be justified in terms of increased trade between the two countries. It would also be feasible at relatively modest investment costs to join up the Nigerian and the Cameroon railways. This idea is related to the linking up of the Ivory Coast, Ghana, Togo, Dahomey, and Nigeria, where, round the Gulf of Benin, there is a heavy concentration of population and prospects of rapid development.

There are three major inter-connexions prima facie feasible and desirable as a basis for an East African economic community, which would also interconnect Central and East Africa.

The first is a road link between Addis Ababa and Nairobi, which is being studied. The second is a link between the copper belt in Zambia and Dar-es-Salaam or a port to the south. There are two possibilities. One is the improvement of the present primitive road link and the other is a railway. Both projects are being studied. The estimated investment cost of the link would be of the order of US $200 million and the improvement of the road would, of course, cost very much less. The justification of the rail link would require a minimum volume of traffic in accordance with the principles already expounded. Once this threshold was reached, transport by rail would be considerably cheaper. An impetus may be the diversion of Zambia's copper from the Rhodesian rail system. A further argument is that potentially rich agricultural country would be opened up in Tanzania, and the exploitation of Tanzania's coal be made possible.

The third area concerns what is known as the Great Lakes area, a project involving the connecting up of the Sudanese, East African, and Congo railway systems.[22] Seven countries are involved: the Sudan, Kenya, Uganda, Tanzania, Rwanda, Burundi, and the Democratic Republic of the Congo. The part of the population of these countries which would form the unified market brought into existence by connecting up the railways is at present about 30 million. The estimated cost is of the order of US $300 million. Traffic of the order of 300,000 tons per annum would be required as an economic justification, which seems not impossible in ten years, particularly if the industrialization perspectives outlined in

Chapter IV are realized. Arising out of this project it should be added that improved road connexions between Burundi and Rwanda and Uganda would be required, the investment cost of which would be relatively small.

This has been no more than an outline sketch of the principal inter-connecting links required to make possible major industrial development programmes in Africa. Some of the projects are under way, others are being studied, and the remainder are no more than hypotheses. Yet the urgency of speeding up progress is apparent. No dogmatic positions are taken as to the mode of transport. There is clearly a place for road, rail, and water. The characteristics and basic economies of each mode are clear.[23]

The total investment cost of developing the African transport system over the next ten to fifteen years in terms of national requirements and new international connexions is not yet known precisely. It has been estimated that the cost of improving to a reasonable level African transport, including ports, airports, railways, and roads, would be of the order of US $4,000 million. This may be compared with a sum of US $9,000 million which has been estimated to have been invested in seven Latin American countries over the past seven years. Other comparisons are: nearly US $47 billion, which has been published as the cost of the inter-State road construction programme only in the United States, and US $3,700 million for the transport sector of the third India five-year plan.[24]

The average percentage of gross investment in transport in Western Europe varies from 17 in the United Kingdom to 30 in Norway. The figure for the United States fell from 28·5 in 1880 to 22 in 1939. Current figures for India and Mexico are of the order of 20 and 27 per cent respectively. This suggests that the proportion is higher in the earlier stages of development. So far as Africa is concerned, much work is in progress but still more has to be done to evaluate seriously the viability of transport projects regarded as prima facie reasonable, taking into account future development prospects, particularly in industry.[25]

## NOTES AND REFERENCES TO CHAPTER VII

[1] Cf. A. B. Mountjoy, *Industrialization of Underdeveloped Countries*, Hutchinson, London, 1963, p. 212: in discussing industrialization, Mountjoy writes, 'In all the examples considered, the concept of the wholeness of a country's economy receives ample justification.' See also his Chapter 6 on environmental and human problems.

[2] See *Report of ECA Mission on Economic Cooperation in Central Africa*, op. cit., Chapter VI.

[3] See in this context Sir John Cockroft, *Technology for Developing Countries*, Overseas Development Institute, London, 1966, which gives an account of the possibilities and work being done concerning the adaptation of industrial technologies to developing countries, and also of the work of the Tropical Products Institute.

[4] Although in a different field, inspiration and guidance can be found from the late Professor Haldane's last paper (see J. B. S. Haldane, 'Biological Research in Developing Countries', *Man and Africa*, CIBA, London, p. 222).

[5] F. Harbison, *High Level Manpower for Nigeria's Future*, Lagos, 1960; *Final Report of Conference of African States on the Development of Education in Africa*, ECA/UNESCO, 1961; *The Development of Higher Education in Africa*, UNESCO, 1962.

[6] Harbison and Myers, *Education, Manpower and Economic Growth*, New York, 1964; Harbison and Myers, *Manpower and Education*, New York, 1965; F. Harbison, 'The African University and Human Resources Development', *Journal of Modern African Studies*, Vol. 3, No. 1.

Surendra Patel has drawn attention to the fact that the educational distance between developed and developing countries is not as large as is sometimes thought, and that in principle the gap could be closed within half a century. See S. J. Patel, 'Educational Distance between Nations', *Indian Economic Journal*, Vol. XIII, No. 1, 1967.

[7] E. J. Berg, 'Senegal, Guinea, Ivory Coast', in Harbison and Myers, *Manpower and Education*, op. cit.

[8] E. J. Berg, ibid., p. 245.

[9] E. J. Berg, ibid, p. 257.

[10] Guy Hunter in Harbison and Myers, *Manpower and Education*, ibid.

[11] W. C. Cash, 'A Critique of Manpower Planning and Educational Change in Africa', *Economic Development and Cultural Change*, Vol. XIV, No. 1, October 1965.

[12] See also E. R. Rado, 'Manpower Education and Economic Growth', *Journal of Modern African Studies*, Vol. 4, No. 1, May 1966. He is somewhat critical of what he of course recognizes to be the pioneer work of Harbison and his colleagues. In particular he suggests that there has been excessive concentration on elimination of shortages of highly skilled manpower at the expense of equally likely surpluses of less skilled manpower, and also that a concentration on manpower and educational needs in numbers is equivalent to a failure to come to grips with the most difficult problem of all, the cost of education.

[13] See E/CN. 14/363, Addis Ababa, 1966; *Science and Technical Education in Africa*, E/CN. 14/398, Addis Ababa, 1967; G. Skorov, *Integration of Educational and Economic Planning in Tanzania*, IIEP, UNESCO, Paris 1966; and G. Hunter, *Manpower, Employment, and Education in the Rural Economy of Tanzania*, IIEP, UNESCO, Paris, 1966.

[14] Speech by President Johnson on Africa Day 1966.

[15] For a detailed educational and manpower survey carried out on behalf of a country, Zambia, see *Economic Development of Zambia* (N'Dola, 1964); report of ECA Mission.

[16] For a succinct account of the principles of carrying out a systematic and

continuous natural resources inventory, see *The Natural Resources Inventory*, prepared for the second United Nations Regional Cartographic Conference for Africa (document E/CN. 14/CART/169), Addis Ababa, July 1966.

[17] Many of the facts presented in this section are derived from P. Sevette, *L'Économie de l'énergie dans les pays en voie de développement*, Presses Universitaires de France, Paris, 1963.

[18] Specific possibilities of co-operation between Ghana and Togo, Ghana and Dahomey, and Ghana and the Ivory Coast are summarized in ECA document E/CN. 14/INR/136.

[19] See the *Report of the ECA Mission on Industrial Co-ordination to Algeria, Libya, Morocco and Tunisia* (E/CN. 14/248).

[20] The approach in this section owes much to the work of Louis Gelineau, Regional Transport Adviser to the Economic Commission for Africa.

[21] Within the context of transport, North Africa, defined for present purposes as Morocco, Algeria, Tunisia, Libya, and the UAR, can be disregarded. There are no communications at present between the north and the south of the Sahara other than air and rough desert tracks, although the UN Special Fund is assisting a Committee composed of Algeria, Tunisia, Mali, and Niger to examine the possibility of a Trans-Sahara transport route.

[22] See 'Industrialization, Economic Co-operation, and Transport: Hypothesis of Work in the Region of the Great African Lakes'; a paper contributed by the Economic Commission for Africa to the Symposium on Industrial Development in Africa held in Cairo in January–February 1966 (document E/CN. 14/AS/IV/7).

[23] In this study nothing is said about airlines. In Africa as in other vast underdeveloped regions, air is bound to play a relatively greater part in the carriage of goods than has been the case in relatively compactly developed regions such as Western Europe. Furthermore, there are perspectives for a long-run fall in the relative costs of traffic of goods by air. The whole process would be facilitated by greater co-operation among African airlines than is at present the case. However, even if an optimistic view is taken of the future of air transport, it can be no substitute for extensive development of surface transport.

[24] See Ian Shannon, 'Aspects of Road Development in Africa', paper contributed to the Fifth World Meeting of the International Road Federation, London, September 1966.

The total investment cost, whatever it is, may well be over-estimated and in this context the lessons of the USSR are of interest. It has been calculated that the capital output ratio in transport in the USSR is of the order of 2:1 compared with 7:1 in the Western world. It is true that much of the difference is explained by less emphasis on passenger traffic on the railways, where more ancillaries for speed and comfort are required. On the other hand, much of the difference is due to intensive use of capital equipment (see H. Hunter, 'Transportation in Soviet Development', included in G. Fromm (ed.), *Transport Investment and Economic Development*, Brookings Institute, Washington, D.C., 1965).

[25] The evaluation of transport projects is a complex question, more difficult than that of industrial projects (see Hans A. Adler, 'Evaluating Transport Projects', *Finance and Development*, IMF and IBRD, Vol. III, No. 1, March 1966). Furthermore, transport links, particularly railways, can legitimately be

established somewhat ahead (although not too far ahead) of foreseeable traffic, since growth is thereby promoted, particularly along the line of rail. There were no feasibility studies before the American railroads pushed westward in the nineteenth century. Somewhat nearer home, the relatively rapid development of Angola can be traced largely to its major railway.

# CHAPTER VIII

# THE AGENTS
# OF INDUSTRIALIZATION

It has been argued that there are three main elements in a strategy of industrial development: the right sort of perspective in the sense of an expanding role for industry and, within this, emphasis on production of intermediate and capital goods capable of changing the structure of the economy; the appropriate prerequisites; and thirdly, the appropriate agents. Chapter I has sketched out, largely in terms of principles, the role of industrialization and Chapter IV has demonstrated the perspectives. Chapter VII has summarized the prerequisites, and this chapter examines the agents or means of industrialization. The perspectives are beginning to be understood although, as has been shown in Chapter V, there is a hard road ahead in negotiating multi-national arrangements. Increasing emphasis is being placed on satisfying the prerequisites, although not enough attention is being paid to the human infrastructure. The third area remains essentially barren. What this means is that not nearly enough recognition has so far been given to the human factor, the realization that in the last analysis it is people who determine any kind of development. This chapter examines in turn industrial planning and programming, project evaluation and preparation, training, demand and the organization of markets, industrial promotion and the institutions involved, and, finally, the role of foreign technical assistance.

## INDUSTRIAL PROGRAMMING AND PLANNING

It is not the intention here to examine the whole problem of development planning,[1] nor to outline a complete industrial plan. It is rather to draw attention to a series of key issues which have to be examined by industrial planners. The issues involved are relatively straightforward, although at present neglected:

Industrial planning has to be recognized as part of development planning, with therefore a long perspective, preferably a series of plans covering fifteen to twenty years.

The basic objectives are both to change the structure and to raise the rate of growth of the economy, necessarily involving diversification and industrialization. Employment creation is in some countries a legitimate objective although, as shown earlier, this is often in conflict with raising the growth rate. A major issue is ways and means of increasing the output per man throughout the economy.

It is essential to obtain a picture of the resources available or capable of being made available in the plan period: raw materials, manpower of different kinds at existing levels of skill, land, physical infrastructure, capital resources in sight—domestic and external—and finally industry already in existence, including excess capacity and scope for better utilization thereof.

A coherent growth framework is required both for a macro-economic programme and the micro-economic programme made up of individual industries.

The relevant coefficients, such as capital intensity, the scope for choice of technology, import coefficients, and shadow pricing have to be established.

Projections of demand are required. There are techniques for estimating demand for consumer goods through current imports, family budgets, the retail trade, and income elasticities of demand. In estimating demand for capital goods, a variety of techniques, some still primitive, have to be used, largely based on the experience of other developing countries, technical coefficients, and trial and error.

Careful calculations have to be made of the precise rate of growth of industry, the kinds of industry feasible, and their respective shares in GDP. In this context the problems of a dual economy arise: one sector concerned with the establishment of basic industries, and the other, at a different technical level, concerned primarily with employment creation, where the experience of Japan is particularly relevant.

Projects have to be prepared or evaluated, a subject which is considered later in this chapter.

There are problems of location and regional development to be considered, and attention has already been drawn to the conflict between the advantages of concentration on growing points and the dangers of neglecting weaker areas.

Provision has to be made for proper manpower planning and training.

There is the role of foreign trade in development plans. On the import side this involves import substitution and also the cutting down of luxury imports so as to use effectively foreign exchange earnings for development purposes. On the export side the limitations on increasing earnings of foreign exchange through the sale of primary products have been discussed and it has been argued that the key issue is export of manufactured goods from one country to another. In a sense this is part of a comprehensive all-African import substitution programme. As Chapter V has brought out, there is a marked contrast between the fortunes of those countries, particularly in North Africa, which have geared their development programme to internally propelled growth, and those, as in West Africa or Ethiopia, which are still relying primarily on export-determined growth.

A serious industrial programme has to regard industry as not simply the promotion of a series of scattered industrial development projects but as something consciously tailored to establishing relationships among industries through external economies and backward and forward linkages. Development has been characterized as 'filling up the blanks in the input–output table'. How this is to be done depends not only on the conception of the industrial development plan but also methods of execution. It is for each country to decide these methods for itself and there is undoubtedly much scope for private enterprise, domestic or foreign. On the other hand, it is difficult to see how a satisfactory and comprehensive programme can be carried through unless the government is ready and able to step in and fill up the gaps.

## PROJECT EVALUATION AND PREPARATION

The subject of project evaluation and preparation has hitherto been a neglected one and also one where there has been considerable confusion, not least of terminology, on which at present there is not yet full agreement. Its importance derives from two points. The first, as has been shown in Chapter VI, is that there is evidence that more finance would have been available for Africa than has been the case, with better preparation of projects. The second, a longer-term consideration, is that African countries are still

primarily dependent on the outside for the preparation of their projects. This discussion is concerned primarily with the preparation
of projects. The same considerations and the same sequence apply
to the proper evaluation of a project. This is just as important, in
view of the dangers involved of being 'sold' non-viable projects,
with dire consequences, as has been seen in Ghana and India.

In this section the terminology and breakdown used by Bryce in
his *Industrial Development* is used.[2] Although it is possible to disagree
with him on aspects of his general strategy of development, and in
particular his strong predilection for private enterprise, he is an
admirable and lucid guide to project preparation. He also rightly
points out that a proper sequence has to be followed irrespective of
whether the project is to be carried out by private or public enterprise.

There are three separate steps in the sequence of project development. First, the preliminary study; secondly, the investigation of feasibility, which in turn falls into three separate parts: a
technical requirements study, a technical feasibility study, and an
economic feasibility study; and thirdly, the engineering studies and
establishment of financial requirements and structure up to the
point where invitations to tender may be sent out. The importance
of observing a proper sequence lies in the fact that the engineering
studies are expensive, accounting for 8 to 15 per cent of the total
project cost, and that premature ordering of equipment may be
still more expensive. If the proper sequence is followed the project
may be abandoned at any of the early stages without undue loss.

The nature of the *preliminary study* is fairly evident. The essential
question is whether prima facie there is a market, and in the first
instance a domestic market, for the products envisaged. This can
be done by analysing the evolution of the existing market through
import statistics together with forward projections on the basis of
assumptions not only as to the market for the product but also as to
the overall growth of the economy. Also within the scope of the
preliminary study is an examination of the prima facie possibilities
of production on the basis of natural and other resources of the
economy. Most of the studies prepared by an organization like the
ECA fall into the category of preliminary studies, although some
of them have gone into considerable detail and depth.

In the *feasibility study* proper there is also a sequence, once again
offering possibilities of abandoning the project at an early stage.

The first step therefore is the *technical requirements study*. The purpose of this is to set out precisely the quantity, quality, and specification of all the inputs required by the project: raw materials, ancillaries, labour, energy, water, transport, etc.; to estimate the total cost and the major items of capital cost, distinguishing between foreign exchange and local currency; and thirdly, to detail estimated production and overhead costs for operating the plant envisaged on the basis of given assumptions of the unit cost per item needed. Also within the scope of the technical requirements study is the question of the range of capacity possible and hence of the economies of scale; and the scope for choice in technology and processes of production. A detailed examination of alternative locations within a country is not within the scope of a technical requirements study, nor of course is the preparation of detailed specifications and engineering drawings. Normally a technical requirements study accounts for about one per cent of the total cost of a project. Nevertheless it is a highly specialized business, usually beyond the scope of personnel available within a developing country.

Assuming that the first two hurdles are successfully negotiated, technical and economic feasibility analyses come next and can be undertaken simultaneously. The *technical feasibility analysis* is required to examine in relation to the actual conditions of the country whether the technical requirements of the industry can be met, in what location, and at what scale of output. Each input has therefore to be assessed in detail in relation to specific locations, both as to quality and cost. The choice of site may depend largely upon transport facilities or the possibility of providing them within reasonable time and at a reasonable cost. The minimum scale of output is frequently crucial, depending on the nature of the industry. On the other hand, there may be alternative scales of output possible and it is part of the business of the technical feasibility study to establish this, including the effect on capital and operating costs. Another crucial question which falls within the scope of this stage of the analysis is the choice of technology, if indeed a choice arises. There are two dangers to be avoided. One is that it is not appropriate to use a developing country as a guinea-pig for an untried technology. The other is that in most cases it is not right to use obsolescent technologies or, which may come to the same thing, to seek an 'intermediate technology'. As has been shown already,

M

in a wide range of capital goods industries and, in particular, process industries such as basic chemicals, there is no real choice of technology. On the other hand, in the operations which are ancillary to the basic process, such as handling, packaging, and sometimes finishing, there is frequently a choice between capital and labour intensive methods. In other industries such as textiles there is a choice between capital and labour intensive methods but there are dangers. Thus, if a developing country envisages exporting textiles in world markets it will not in general be able to avoid modern machinery, even despite low labour costs. The essence of the case for adopting a fully modern technology, except in areas where there is a real and legitimate choice, is first that the whole purpose of laying down basic industry, intermediate and capital goods, is to transform the structure of the economy and raise the productivity of all sectors thereof. This aim is defeated if semi-obsolete equipment is used. The second point is that frequently the most up-to-date equipment is skill-saving and it is skill which is, at this stage, Africa's scarcest factor. Within these basic principles, however, there is clearly scope for much more research on development or adaptation of appropriate technologies for African conditions.

Much of the technical feasibility study analysis should be capable of being carried out by a country's own staff. The training of specialists in this job is considered further later in this chapter. Where resort is made to outside assistance it is essential to avoid employing those who are likely later to be interested in selling equipment or services.

The *economic feasibility analysis* is concerned primarily with assessing commercial, national, and multi-national economic profitability. The essential problem is to determine the size of the market, to project its growth, and, where there is actual or potential competition, domestic or foreign, to assess what share of the market can be obtained. The technical feasibility analysis will have established in detail estimated production costs, which provide the basis for estimates of earnings and commercial and social profitability. It is part of the economic feasibility analysis to compare the cost advantages or disadvantages of the proposed project with those of competitors, actual or potential. This in turn leads to the problem of first assessing commercial profitability and then adjusting where appropriate from the overall national or multi-national point of view. In assessing commercial profitability there are two main dangers: the first is that some of the relevant items are forgotten; and the other is over-optimism based on experience in developed countries. Capital costs have to be estimated in detail distinguishing between foreign exchange and local currency requirements. Working capital has to be estimated. Sales revenues have to be calculated. But the calculation of operating costs presents particular difficulties. It is not in general too difficult to work out raw material costs. Labour costs are almost invariably underestimated in the initial stages of establishing new plants in developed countries. Maintenance costs, both labour and spare parts, are also frequently underestimated. Two other points should be mentioned. One is that allowance has to be made for depreciation even though this is not a cash expense. The other is that proper estimates have to be made of what is known as the 'cash flow'. This cash is needed during the construction phase when no revenue is coming in. After operations start cash will be needed for initial working capital. The plant will not reach full-scale working for a considerable period after it makes a start, yet cash will be needed and revenue will be flowing in at well below the rate of outflow. All this has to be carefully phased in advance.

The starting-point is and must be commercial profitability during the whole of the revenue-earning life of the equipment before adjustments can be made from the point of view of national economic profitability. Thus the real cost to the economy may be greater or less than the cost to the enterprise. The main reason why private profitability calculations deviate from social profitability calculations in developing countries is that prevailing market prices deviate from equilibrium or shadow prices. There are two main types of example: one concerns factor prices, such as labour and capital, which are relevant to factor proportions and the choice of technology. Given equilibrium prices and supplies of factors the economic process of production is determined, but this may not be the feasible solution in practice. On the second point, foreign exchange, the currencies of developing countries are generally over-valued and become more so as development proceeds. Foreign exchange rates can thus become the decisive factor in the choice between domestic production and imports.

Examples of legitimate adjustment in operating costs are that duty may be charged on raw materials which are costs to the enterprise but not to the economy. Resources will be drawn upon, e.g. spare electric power capacity which should be properly charged to the enterprise but which represents no cost to the economy. The most difficult problem arises in relation to labour. It is now well established that it is legitimate to protect a new infant industry during the initial period of its operation. It is now also being recognized that this argument is powerfully and independently reinforced by another, i.e. when the labour drawn upon is either unemployed or under-employed, yet the enterprise has to pay the going rate. From a national point of view labour costs are lower than wages or even nil. The use of what are known as shadow or equilibrium prices is difficult in practice, as already pointed out. Opportunity cost may be zero, but there is still a social cost.

Similarly adjustments can be made to operating income estimates. The income of an enterprise is derived from the revenue from sales. Yet the benefit to the economy may be greater, e.g. when the project earns foreign exchange or saves foreign exchange through import substitution, or when human skills are created and incomes from new jobs are gained year after year.

There is another major point, which is still more difficult to calculate in practice. The setting up of a new plant is likely to lead to a whole range of external economies through linkage effects, i.e. the establishment of one plant which either produces the inter-industry inputs for another or buys its own inputs from another; where new infrastructural facilities are established which lower costs and in turn make other enterprises possible; and perhaps most important of all in a developing country, where management and labour are trained and a new climate of industrial development begins to be established.

As with the technical feasibility analysis, much of the economic feasibility analysis should be capable of being carried out by a country's own staff within a reasonable time. In most African countries such facilities are lacking, but could and should be provided as a matter of urgency.

The last preparatory stage in industrial development, assuming that both technical and economic feasibility are now established, is the most expensive of all; the preparation of *detailed engineering designs, drawings, and specifications* frequently requiring still further specialized investigation. This work falls into three main parts: the first relates to the site and includes soil and foundation testing, water analysis and supply, detailed plans for plant lay-out and transport, and drainage and waste disposal; the second stage is the design of the precise equipment, together with the preparation of detailed drawings and specifications; the third part is the design of structures and of all remaining non-process mechanical and general engineering works, together with preparation of detailed plans and specifications. All this leads to a detailed list of requirements of equipment and spare parts. In addition, of course, a detailed time schedule is required for stages of construction, of installation, and of ordering and delivery of equipment. As part of this stage in the project preparation, requests for tenders have to be drawn up; the requests have to be distributed to potential suppliers; the tenders received have to be analysed from a technical and financial point of view; and recommendations for purchase have to be made. Finally, parallel with all this work emerges a detailed total project cost and a detailed financial structure.

In this last stage of the operation the normal practice is to employ a specialized independent engineering consultant who will also have the task of supervising construction and final inspection. The consulting engineer is the representative of the project owner and must, of course, be entirely independent of the contractor or contractors who are awarded the job of carrying through the project itself. For some time to come in Africa consulting engineers, at least for projects of any size, have to be obtained from developed countries.

A country cannot be said to be genuinely industrialized until it is in a position to determine in detail its own industrial fate. It has been seen that, in the sequence of project development, most of the vital steps are not in the hands of Africans but of foreigners. Dependence is almost complete in the case of the technical requirements study and the final phase of engineering studies. It is partial and sometimes almost complete, depending on the country, in the case of technical and economic feasibility analyses. Consequently, parallel with the process of carrying through project preparation in all its phases, a massive effort is required immediately to train Africans in all phases of project evaluation and preparation. One approach which is now being pursued jointly by the ECA and the United Nations Industrial Development Organization is specialized courses in project evaluation and preparation. Another possibility would be to associate Africans with foreign teams who are carrying out project studies. A third, which is beginning to be taken in some African countries, is the setting up of a national industrial advisory service. Sometimes such a service could serve several neighbouring countries. These might have a number of functions, but one of them would be to take part in, and train African counterparts in, project evaluation and preparation.

TRAINING

A training programme has to begin with a manpower budget and it has already been shown that both the efforts made so far and the machinery for manpower planning are deficient. Few countries have made any serious projections of manpower requirements and where this has been done the figures relate to global employment targets by broad sectors, without going into the kind of detail by skills which is obviously necessary for industrialization. Less than half of African countries have made surveys of manpower needs, even approximate in character, and of these the more serious relate, as might be expected, to the countries (described in Chapter II) which have drawn up respectable comprehensive development plans. The ECA has made broad estimates of trained manpower required for industrial development in Africa up to 1975 on what appears to be a fairly conservative basis. Nevertheless, the magnitude of the figures (expressed in thousands) speaks for itself (Table 6).

The gap between requirements of manpower for industrial development and what is likely to become available, allowing for existing training machinery, wherever it may be, is such that training on the job must play a major part. Training within industry includes apprenticeship, accelerated training of technicians and craftsmen, training of middle- and high-level management, and methods of disseminating or adapting knowledge about appropriate technologies. In the next decade or so it is inevitable that much of the responsibility for and cost of such training must fall on large employers in both the public and private sectors. To some extent this is bound to involve a direct charge on public funds. For the rest, suitable incentives have to be devised, both to the employer and worker.

Another valuable approach to accelerated training is what is known as guided job experience, both for university graduates and for those already employed who show potential for advancement.

Table 6

TRAINED MANPOWER ESTIMATES FOR INDUSTRIAL DEVELOPMENT

| Sub-Region | Assumed Relative Demand (b) | Management and Supervision | | | Scientists, Engineers, and Technologists | | | Technicians and Foremen | | | Skilled and Semi-skilled Workers | | |
|---|---|---|---|---|---|---|---|---|---|---|---|---|---|
| | | Net Addition to Stock | Replacement of Existing Stock at 5% p.a. | Total to be Trained by 1975 | Net Addition to Stock | Replacement of Existing Stock at 5% p.a. | Total to be Trained by 1975 | Net Addition to Stock | Replacement of Existing Stock at 3½% p.a. | Total to be Trained by 1975 | Net Addition to Stock | Replacement of Existing Stock at 2½% p.a. | Total to be Trained |
| North Africa | 7 | 7·7 | 3·5 | 11·2 | 13·8 | 6·3 | 20·1 | 33·0 | 10·5 | 43·5 | 545·4 | 124·3 | 669·7 |
| West Africa | 5 | 5·5 | 2·5 | 8·0 | 9·9 | 4·5 | 14·4 | 23·6 | 7·5 | 31·1 | 389·6 | 88·8 | 478·4 |
| Central Africa | 2 | 2·2 | 1·0 | 3·2 | 3·9 | 1·8 | 5·7 | 9·4 | 3·0 | 12·4 | 155·8 | 35·5 | 191·3 |
| East Africa | 4 | 4·4 | 2·0 | 6·4 | 7·9 | 3·6 | 11·5 | 18·9 | 6·0 | 24·9 | 311·7 | 71·0 | 382·7 |
| Regional Total (a) | | 19·8 | 9·0 | 28·8 | 35·5 | 16·2 | 51·7 | 84·9 | 27·0 | 111·9 | 1402·5 | 319·6 | 1722·1 |

(a) Excluding the Republic of South Africa.

(b) Relative ratios of projected GDP for 1965 with some adjustment downward for North and West Africa.

Source: Some Aspects of Manpower Requirements and the Training of Technical and Managerial Personnel for Industrial Development (E/CN. 14/AS/IV/9), Table 3.

This can be done partly within the framework of training within industry programmes and at a variety of levels; partly by vacation courses for students grounded in science and technology; and partly through programmes organized by the International Association for the Exchange of Students for Technical Experience (IAESTE) and other similar international associations. Well-organized study tours such as those arranged by the United Nations can also play a part.

This leads to the role of international technical assistance in the training process. To some extent this is done through technical assistance programmes, whether organized by the UN agencies or bilaterally, but these programmes appear to have been less successful than they might be, owing to insufficient attention to the finding of suitable African counterparts. The experts, therefore, in many cases perform a useful function while in the country, but leave little behind.

Both the UN agencies, and still more the bilateral technical assistance programmes, provide extensively for training of Africans abroad. There can be no doubt that this is valuable for higher personnel, whether in science and technology or in management, but there tends to be an indiscriminate element in these programmes. Candidates are not always suitably qualified. There is insufficient supervision of the trainees while abroad and those who are trained sometimes fail to return or, when they do, find themselves in other occupations. An attempt to improve the situation is being made by UNESCO and the ECA, in association with the donor countries. More important still, large numbers of Africans find their way abroad on training courses of varying content and duration who could be better trained in their own or another African country.

It is being increasingly recognized that much more training in all fields, and particularly in industry, can and should be carried out in Africa through intra-African co-operation. Reference has already been made to how this process could be given much more impetus at university level through greater specialization among African universities. In addition, a number of countries already have specialized training schools inadequately utilized. More could be done by those countries which have already installed substantial industrial works, to receive for training within industry nationals of neighbouring countries.

Looking next at the problem of industrial training in more detail, the first point to be made is the degree of detailed breakdown required, by level and types of skill and by industrial branches. Secondly, it should be recognized that although little or nothing can be done to shorten the period of training at the highest levels of skill, whether in management or in science and technology, much is possible to compress the period of training at the middle level. This has been shown to be the case both in the developed countries in recent years and in such under-developed countries as have recently made real progress, such as Mexico, India, and the UAR.

Finally, a word should be said about the special problems of management of industrial enterprises. In an under-developed economy this is inevitably the weakest link in the chain, for understandable reasons, not least the environment.[3] As a United Nations report has put it:

The unfavourable features are well known, lack of external economies due to inadequate economic and social overheads, scarcity of skills, and a social structure and pattern of behaviour characteristic in many cases of a pre-industrial society. Thus, the typical manager in an under-developed country, in addition to his conventional managerial duties, has constantly to adjust to, and allow for, the inadequacies of his environment. He has to improvise, provide solutions and, in particular, compensate for the lack of many facilities which, in a developed country, are available as 'free goods' and often taken for granted by his counterpart there.[4]

The same report makes a number of suggestions for action which would still seem to be valid. One is further study of the transition from personnel to functional management and in particular the structure and functions of management in public enterprises. This is evidently of great importance in Africa, where there are no grounds for attempting to distinguish between management of public and private enterprise in training programmes and where the civil servant should clearly be trained also in business management, in view of the functions he has to perform. A further point is that the bilateral technical assistance programmes appear to be devoting insufficient attention to management training. There are also recommendations relating to the need for proper manuals, for training in quality control procedures, for training of maintenance personnel, and for devoting much more attention to the problem of distribution as a necessary function of management and one which is often neglected in developing countries.[5]

The problem is a vast one and apart from the greater contribution which could be made from training abroad, there may be a case for tackling the problem within Africa on two fronts: one, the establishment of a management training institute; and the other, comprehensive and regular short-term courses for those already established but insufficiently trained, perhaps organized on a sub-regional basis.

### DEMAND AND THE ORGANIZATION OF MARKETS

Perhaps because the limitations of import substitution have been insignificantly recognized, and perhaps also because most African countries have opted for some form of development planning without, as a rule, paying much attention to machinery for executing the plan, the market problem seems to have been neglected in Africa. This is not, of course, the case where production is primarily for export overseas or where production of consumer goods is firmly in the hands of foreign enterprise. Yet if, as has been argued in this study, the main task now is to establish production of intermediate and capital goods within the grouping of countries, much more thought will have to be given to creating organized demand.

One aspect, and indeed an obvious one, is market research, itself related to the problem of project preparation discussed earlier in this chapter. There is no need to go into detail here. What is required is relatively straightforward and if the importance of the subject is recognized, the necessary techniques can be taught, and learnt, fairly quickly.

More difficult is the creation of demand for the products of new industries deliberately established on a multi-national basis. It has already been shown, in an earlier chapter, that one of the obstacles to the setting up of an iron and steel plant in Liberia to serve several West African countries has been an inability among the potential customers to agree to take up, on a regular and long-term basis, a sufficient proportion of the potential output of the plant envisaged. Manifestly it is asking a lot to expect this to be done in the case of a single industry; the more multilateral industries there are established in a given area, the easier it should be to arrive at firm multilateral agreements.

It has to be recognized that a customs union, a free-trade area, a common market, or any variant of these devices is in itself quite insufficient. There have to be firm long-term purchase agreements among the consumers and multilateral producing plants and it would seem that the prospects of arriving at such agreements would be facilitated by the establishment of sub-regional industrial authorities for each of the multi-national industries, representative of both producers and consumers. Indeed, such authorities might be empowered to go a step farther and regulate the volume of imports from outside the sub-region of the industrial product in question, and the terms on which such imports are obtained.

It would be out of place to attempt to go into further detail here. Each case has to be worked out on its own merits, a laborious and detailed task. It is sufficient to stress here that, without attention to the organization of markets and what is in effect the creation of demand, there can be little prospect of carrying through the industrial development strategy which has been outlined and which is becoming increasingly the professed policy of most African governments.

### INDUSTRIAL PROMOTION

Finance is clearly a major element in the promotion of industrial development, but there is no need to repeat here the arguments already set out in Chapter VI. What remains to be considered is various institutional instruments.

Earlier in this chapter there has been some discussion of the need and scope for industrial research and it has been suggested that in most African countries this has to be on a grouped basis, although there is more than one possible approach. But industrial research arrangements are unlikely to be of much interest to countries which have no national promotion arrangements and it is unfortunately the case that few African countries have established or indeed fully appreciate the need for national machinery. The functions which it would seem such machinery—and it may be that more than one organ is required—should carry out may be summarized as follows:

1. To advise on industrial planning and programming.

2. To advise on the selection of projects, in particular proposals from foreign private investors, in other words, undertake project evaluation.
3. To advise on the need for and commissioning of feasibility studies, and begin itself to carry out feasibility studies for smaller enterprises, i.e. the project preparation process.
4. To advise on application for tariff protection in the industrial field.
5. To advise on sources of industrial finance, public or private.
6. To carry out market research.
7. To advise on industrial legislation.
8. To promote industrial training.
9. To advise on development of African entrepreneurship, including the setting up of industrial estates, and to carry out or promote industrial extension work.
10. To advise on standardization.
11. To advise on marketing, including export promotion.

A vital part of the service or services should be the training of counterparts in all these fields and, above all, in the evaluation of industrial projects and their preparation.

Something along these lines exists in the North African countries and, with the help of the United Nations Development Programme, is being established in a limited number of others, e.g. Tanzania, but there is a long way to go.

Another useful instrument is the national development corporation. This can take a number of different forms and there are examples in almost all the ex-British African territories. Fundamentally, it is a device for State intervention in industrial development under largely autonomous conditions and with the flexibility of management which can be expected if day-to-day control by a government department is avoided. The corporation may confine itself to looking for and helping to prepare industrial projects and making finance available to the private sector on reasonably easy terms. It may go still farther and take a direct part in the establishment and management of industry, including assuming the entrepreneurial function by taking risks. This has been the case in Uganda, which is generally agreed to have been the most successful of the development corporations in Africa. Its experience has not been universally good, but this is in the nature of risk-taking.[6]

It would be rash to generalize on the development corporation from one relative success, and a series of other distinctly cautious experiments, as to the value of substantial State participation in industrial development. There are two less successful experiences in Nigeria, one concerned with timber, at Sapele, and the other with groundnut crushing, at Kano. It has been shown that productivity, per acre or per ton in plantations administered by development corporations concerned with these sectors, has been superior to that in peasant holdings, but that this was largely offset by high expenses in capital and administration. In addition, the share of incomes generated spent on imports was greater than with peasant production, thus limiting the indirect economic effects. On the other hand, peasant farming and food processing encouraged in Northern Nigeria generated incomes spent largely on local manufacture. It has been shown that although the Cameroon Development Corporation operating in the former British Southern Cameroons and now in the Republic of the Cameroon may have overreached itself recently, it made a useful contribution to cooperative marketing and extension of credit. It can also be argued that these corporations have had a good record in continuity of employment and avoidance of absenteeism comparable to experience in Europe or the United States.[7] It is evident that experience of development corporations is mixed and insufficient as yet to draw further conclusions. Yet their potential, if operated on an imaginative and energetic basis, as in Uganda, is considerable.

The experience, for good or ill, of the development corporation leads on to the role of government in industrial development. It has already been seen that most African governments are attached to the principle of the mixed economy, although this concept is a cloudy one and variously interpreted. At this stage of African experience three points would seem to be clear. The first is that there is a case for any form of enterprise, public or private, domestic or foreign, which can make a genuine contribution to development. The second is a sheer lack of skills capable of conceiving and preparing projects and managing and running industrial enterprises. Such skills have to be created and there can be no serious prospects of their appearing spontaneously. African governments are bound to play a part in creating and training such skills and since they are bound to be scarce for a long time to come, they have to be judiciously and carefully employed. This in itself is an argument for a major State sector. The third point, which is a related one, is that all the arguments of principle and of experience in developing countries, whether in Africa or elsewhere, are such that it is unlikely that a serious strategy of industrial development can be devised and applied without extensive government intervention.

There remains the much discussed question of the promotion of African entrepreneurship. In the perspective of world history, it may be seen that private capitalism has arisen and prospered over a relatively short period of time, at most two centuries, and in a relatively small number of countries. The conditions which have made possible the emergence of such a system, and in particular the ability to obtain command of significant savings and to apply them to industrial enterprise, are simply not present, save on a limited scale, in most of the world's at present under-developed countries. That every effort should be made to encourage entrepreneurship is only reasonable, but it would be an illusion to suppose that the mechanisms which have led to the high levels of development in North America and Western Europe are likely to be present in Africa. There is, indeed, much confusion of thought on the subject. Experience shows, not only in Africa but still more in Asia and Latin America, that the fact that a man can amass or control significant sums of money is no guarantee that he will be able to generate productive enterprise. It is unfortunately more likely that he will become a money-lender or speculate in real estate.

Much of the current argument for small-scale industry is based, consciously or unconsciously, on the belief that this is a means of promoting entrepreneurship. Some of the confusion underlying this discussion has been examined in Chapter I and it has been shown that such a strategy is, in itself, unlikely to lead to real industrial development. But this is far from saying that there is not an important place for small industry in a coherent strategy.[8] One institutional device which clearly merits attention is the industrial estate, which, apart from doing something to train and facilitate the activities of domestic enterprises, can give at relatively small investment cost an impetus to small industries with growth capacity, through the provision for the application and development of appropriate technologies; and combine public and private enterprise.

## THE ROLE OF TECHNICAL ASSISTANCE

Technical assistance is provided from a wide variety of both multi-lateral and bilateral sources and it is in the nature of things that co-ordination is difficult and limited. It is useful in assessing needs to distinguish between the short and the long run and then to examine which types of agency are best fitted to supply the different kinds of services required.

In the short run, further progress in industrialization in Africa depends to a marked degree on the carrying out of feasibility and engineering studies designed to translate the potential industrial opportunities revealed by the many preliminary studies carried out in recent years into specific industrial projects. Financing is the final stage and this question has already been discussed in an earlier chapter. But before finance can be attracted or usefully employed, the project has to be fully prepared in all its stages. There are two sources of assistance. One is the UNDP, through its Special Fund. This has hitherto concentrated primarily on infrastructure, surveys, and training, and is only now beginning to place more emphasis on industrial projects. However, its resources are necessarily limited and, as an additional source, it should now be possible to draw massively on bilateral donor countries for the preparation of feasibility and engineering studies. Although it is evident that the support of the governments of these countries is required, the main burden is bound to fall on the private sector and this, indeed, is an advantage, since engineering studies, at least, are not generally carried out unless the subsequent financing is broadly assured. One danger is that African countries may be tempted to confine themselves to providing shopping lists rather than ensure that, when they seek outside assistance in this way, the projects chosen are consistent with a coherent development strategy and development plan. Furthermore, increasing efforts are now required to attract outside assistance for multi-national projects. The climate of opinion in the developed countries is moving in this direction so far as Africa is concerned.

Again within a short- or perhaps medium-term perspective, much can be done by sending experts to advise African governments on how to strengthen their own machinery in the formulation of industrial policy, industrial programming, and the establishment of institutions for the promotion of industrial development, including ministries of industry, industrial development corporations, industrial development banks, industrial estates, and, above all, industrial advisory and promotion machinery, particularly in the field of project advisory services. This area would appear to be specially appropriate to the UNDP, particularly after its recent reorganization, and also the newly created UN Industrial Development Organization. Needless to say, the bilateral donors can also do much in this area, but the leading role belongs primarily to the international agencies.

The longer-run problems are mainly concerned with training of all kinds. There is a short-run aspect through courses of limited duration organized primarily for those already in responsible positions in African countries who cannot be spared from their jobs for long periods of time, and something is already being done here by international agencies, often with bilateral support. However, if the vast intake of trained manpower indicated as required earlier in this chapter is to be realized, the perspectives have to be conceived over two or three decades. Partly, this means the strengthening of existing institutions and the creation of new ones, necessarily requiring extensive external technical assistance. Partly it also means the willingness of the advanced countries to supply personnel for fairly long periods as advisers and teachers. The rapid process of Africanization in recent years has rightly meant that the key positions in government and the civil service are now in domestic hands, but this is not yet true of technical services, and in particular of the management and day-to-day running of industry. If the process of Africanization is to continue down the line, it is evident that the emphasis, so far as foreign personnel is concerned, must be on advisory and, still more, training roles.

## NOTES AND REFERENCES TO CHAPTER VIII

[1] The literature on development planning is now abundant but it may be useful to refer to four recent contributions: W. A. Lewis, *Development Planning*, London, 1966; A. Waterston, 'A Hard Look at Development Planning', *Finance and Development*, Vol. III. No. 2, 1966 (which points out rightly that long-range planning is of little value unless a valid plan for the next year or two can be drawn up); H. Leroux, '*Analyse critique des programmes de développement*', *Cahiers économiques et sociaux*, Vol. IV, No. 3, Université Lovanium, Kinshasa, October 1966; and C. Coméliau, '*La planification en économie de marche*', ibid.

² Murray D. Bryce, *Industrial Development*, McGraw-Hill, New York, 1960.

³ A study of Puerto Rico (L. G. Reynolds and P. Gregory, *Wages, Productivity and Industrialization in Puerto Rico*, Irwin, Homewood, IU:, 1965) shows the importance of management. Variations in productivity of two and three times and of turnover per annum from less than 10 to 200 per cent are traced to variations in management capacity. Almost one-half of the plant managers had little or no previous experience.

⁴ *Management of Industrial Enterprises in Under-developed Countries*, United Nations (Sales No. 58. II. B.5), New York, p. 1.

⁵ Ibid., pp. 32-34.

⁶ J. T. Simpson, 'Financing of Industrial Development with Particular Reference to Africa' (CID/SYMP. B/11), paper presented to the Symposium on Industrial Development in Africa, Cairo, January–February 1966. The Pakistan Industrial Development Corporation has been a major element in the industrial expansion of the country, sometimes assisting private enterprise but also financing and managing industries itself.

⁷ F. A. Wells and W. A. Warmington, *Studies in Industrialization: Nigeria and the Cameroons*, London, 1962.

⁸ See Staley and Morse, op. cit.

N

## CHAPTER IX

# SOME CONCLUSIONS

In a short book, the primary purpose of which has been to attempt to put the problem of industrial development in Africa in perspective and to show how many aspects have to be taken into account, it would be out of place to set out systematic conclusions or to attempt to summarize an already highly compressed argument.

The wide-ranging industrial perspectives have been shown and have indeed become familiar in recent years. It is now beginning to be realized that present levels of development in Western Europe could be attained by Africa by the beginning of the next century. How far, if this were to be achieved, it would close the gap between the advanced and the developing world is another matter.[1] What is more significant and has been the main thesis of this book, is that perspectives alone, however reasonable, are not enough. It is not a question of any kind of industry but of industries which, through their linkage effects, lead to other industries and add to the real capital of society—in other words, intermediate and capital goods. This in turn, given the size of most African markets and the importance of economies of scale, requires grouping of African countries in joint programmes of industrial development. Large amounts of finance are required and although some of this has to come from abroad, where possible in the form of soft loans or grants, the bulk has to be found within Africa, and can be found.

There are essential prerequisites of industrial development: the application and adaptation of science and technology; education; manpower planning; more systematic efforts to discover economically exploitable natural resources, especially for African markets; energy; and transport.

Still more important are the agents of industrialization: trained manpower at all levels, industrial research, proper project preparation and training in this process, and domestic institutions and machinery for industrial promotion.

This study has attempted to throw some light on which of the African countries have been or are likely to become successful and the reasons why, with, as the other side of the medal, the large number which are tending to stagnate. Two countries have been shown to have found a promising road ahead, the UAR and Tunisia. The first of these has the advantage of a relatively large market. It has launched into industries which are already transforming the structure of the economy and, while there is an active class of entrepreneurs, the State has established strong machinery not only for planning its economy but for executing its plans. There is also great emphasis on the training of manpower for industry. Tunisia is working along similar lines, though it is farther behind and is also greatly handicapped by the small size of the country. In this context it is perhaps the most positive promoter of the grouping of the four Maghreb countries. The Maghreb institutions for promotion of economic co-operation are more advanced than elsewhere in Africa. Given the relatively developed industrial structure of Morocco, the social dynamism in Algeria despite, or perhaps because of, its handicaps in recent years, and the natural wealth of Libya, the prospects of achieving real economic advance in the Maghreb over the next two or three decades, necessarily in large measure through industrial development, seem to be promising.

Another grouping where there is genuine potential is in the four countries of the Senegal River Basin: Guinea, Mali, Mauritania, and Senegal. A coherent strategy of industrial development has yet to be worked out and applied, and despite the encouraging signs of dynamism in two of the countries, Guinea and Mali, genuine agreement on economic co-operation among these countries may still be some way off. And it is disappointing that Guinea seems to be holding back, on ideological grounds.

Farther down the West Coast there are three countries in which, in different ways, there has been appreciable industrial development: Ghana, the Ivory Coast, and Nigeria. Ghana has made progress in education and training and towards the planning of its economy. This is much less true of Nigeria, and hardly the case at all in the Ivory Coast. Furthermore, in the whole of this area of West Africa little has yet been done towards genuine economic co-operation.

In Central Africa there is machinery in five countries: the Republic of the Congo, Gabon, Chad, the Central African Republic, and the Cameroon, which have established a customs union and a common fiscal policy. Potentially, the institutions for a common approach to development are there, but so far little has been done and all these countries remain dependent largely on the exterior in the running of their economies. The same is largely true also of their neighbour, the Democratic Republic of the Congo. Although thinking is changing, it will take time before a full-scale association in Central Africa is likely to be realized.

Despite the difficulties which relate to the breakdown or weakening of former economic associations, i.e. the former Federation of Rhodesia and Nyasaland and former British East Africa, there is now a new East African economic community, which may become the nucleus of something wider still. On the other hand, there is no common approach to a strategy of development in the wider East Africa, particularly in the industrial field, so that these economies also remain largely dependent on external forces. The exceptions may be Tanzania and Uganda, if the perspectives in their comparatively radical development plans can be realized.

The brief survey given in this book of the actual experience of African countries, reinforced, of course, by that of others outside Africa now launched on the development process, would seem to confirm amply the appropriateness of the approach to industrialization which has been argued.

Yet all this is clearly not enough. More knowledge and greater insights are clearly required to account for the disappointing and disturbed experience of so many African countries in the last few years.

Not least is this true of the failure so far to get to grips with real negotiations on economic co-operation, and joint planning. Partly this seems to be lack of clarity as to the vital need for and benefits from the grouping of efforts, and how to set about it. Partly it is the legitimate fears of the weaker brethren. Yet it is the case that while all African conferences stress the need for co-operation and unity and there is a readiness to make institutional agreements, there is a lack of a sense of urgency and engagement when it comes to negotiating, for example, the siting of a new factory.

It would be inappropriate in a work of this kind[2] to attempt to deal directly with political forces, cross-currents, and systems, and indeed, in the present context, unnecessary. If one thing is clear, it is that Africa is neither willing, nor can expect, to gain anything from the simple importation of either of the two conflicting ideologies of the world—capitalism as it has emerged in North

America and Western Europe, and socialism as it is practised in Eastern Europe or China. That much of Africa is still economically dependent on the exterior—this is true of many of the countries specifically examined here, and *a fortiori* still more true of the countries hardly examined—is a fact. The whole tenor of the argument put forward is ways and means of removing external dependence so that African countries can be in a position to manage themselves their own economies. The present state of affairs is called by some 'neo-colonialism'. But to harp on this theme can be seen increasingly to be a sterile approach, with little positive content for economic development and of no more value than that advocated by those who would wish to import, lock, stock, and barrel, one or other of the leading ideologies.

Religious and racial, as well as social and economic, divisions in Africa are real enough. There is growing dissatisfaction with corruption and frequently therefore with the role of the 'leader'. That this sometimes leads to violence, and even to the philosophical justification thereof, is not surprising.[3] There must be diminishing hope, for example, that those parts of South Africa which remain under white South African, Portuguese, or white Rhodesian domination can attain freedom without violence. Yet most of Africa has attained political independence and has now to achieve the counterpart in the economic field. In the nature of things, this task cannot be accomplished in conditions of riot and instability.

Yet there are powerful political and social obstacles standing in the way, a discussion of which is outside the scope of this book. Serious research is required into the real nature of these political and social forces, going well beyond conventional analysis of social welfare and community development, with a view to establishing the economic and social classes which are or can become a positive force in development, in fact, a sociology of development. Without this, the study of African industrial development must remain seriously incomplete.

## NOTES AND REFERENCES TO CHAPTER IX

[1] It is sometimes suggested that, provided there is steady development in Africa, it is of no great moment whether the gap is closed. Dudley Seers takes a different view, arguing that the continuance of a large gap, and still more the

widening thereof, feeds the mechanisms of what he calls the transmission of inequality, with, quite apart from the political consequences, serious adverse effects on the development process (see Dudley Seers, 'The Transmission of Inequality', op. cit.).

² By an international civil servant.

³ A passionate and sincere statement of this point of view can be found in Frantz Fanon, *Les Damnés de la terre*, Paris, 1961.

# GLOSSARY OF ABBREVIATIONS

## UNITED NATIONS ORGANS

ECA: Economic Commission for Africa

ECE: Economic Commission for Europe

ECAFE: Economic Commission for Asia and the Far East

ECLA: Economic Commission for Latin America

FAO: Food and Agriculture Organization

WHO: World Health Organization

UNDP: United Nations Development Programme

UNESCO: United Nations Educational, Scientific and Cultural Organization

UNCTAD: United Nations Conference on Trade and Development

## NATIONAL AND INTERNATIONAL BODIES

USDA: United States Department of Agriculture

EACSO: East African Common Services Organization

ISEA: Institut de science économique appliquée

IDEP: Institut de développement économique et de planification (Dakar)—under ECA auspices

IRES: Institut de recherches économiques et sociales (Lovanium University, Kinshasa)

LAFTA: Latin America Free Trade Area

EEC: European Economic Community

EFTA: European Free Trade Area

COMECON: Council for Mutual Economic Assistance

UDEAC: Union douanière et économique de l'Afrique centrale

ADB: African Development Bank

OECD: Organization for Economic Co-operation and Development

IBRD: International Bank for Reconstruction and Development

IMF: International Monetary Fund

FAC: Fonds aide et co-opération

FED: Fonds européen de développement

IAESTE: International Association for the Exchange of Students for Technical Experience

US AID: United States Agency for International Development

## OTHER ABBREVIATIONS USED

GDP: Gross domestic product

GNP: Gross national product

t/p.a.: tons per annum

ICOR: incremental capital output ratio

## CURRENCIES

As far as possible all values are expressed in US dollars.
$2·4 = one pound sterling.
250 CFA francs = 1 US dollar.

## TONS

All tons are metric tons.

# INDEX

Africa, South, 6, 7, 97, 138, 139, 179
African Development Bank, 124
African Fiscal Programme. *See* Fiscal
   policy
Agriculture, aid for, 125; change in
   growth rate, 62, 63, 64; compared
   with Western Europe, 13; competition in, 100; in Ivory Coast, 39; in
   Kenya, 31; production, 6, 21
Aid, 113, 121–5; and economic
   development, 11; FED programme,
   122; improving distribution of,
   121–2; technical assistance, 123–4.
   *See also* United Nations
Akosombo Dam, 43, 139, 140
Algeria, 6, 22, 89, 92, 140, 177; ammonia production, 77; petroleum in,
   3; plastics industry, 80; industrial
   progress, 25
Alliance for Progress, 123
Aluminium, 3, 32–3, 66, 70–1, 94,
   130, 140
America, Central, efforts towards
   integration, 102
America, Latin, 51–6, 101–4, 138,
   151; dependence on private enterprise, 55; economic intergration in,
   102–4; and economies of scale, 55;
   effects of increased agricultural
   output, 53; fiscal policy, 120;
   production of consumer goods, 52,
   103; purchasing power of exports,
   53; transport equipment industry,
   86; unequal distribution of income,
   52, 119. *See also* ECLA *and* Import
   substitution
America, North, 2, 138, 179
Amin, Samir, 34, 40–1
Ammonia, 77, 79
Angola, 6, 146
Argentina, 8, 51, 52, 53, 54
Asia, 101, 114

Asian Development Bank, 101
Aswan Dam, 139, 140

Baer, W., 8
Balance of payments, 5, 46, 113, 114
Berg, E. J., 132, 135
Bolivia, 52
Botswana, 24
Brazil, 8–9, 51, 52, 54
Bryce, Murray D., 158
Building materials industry, 74–6;
   cement, 74, 94; glass, 75; need for
   sub-regional co-operation, 75
Bulgaria, 106
Burma, 133
Burundi, 6, 22, 92, 93; lack of
   industrialization in, 24; natural gas
   prospects, 77; transport in, 150, 151

Cameroon, 6, 32–3, 117, 140; cement
   production, 75; Development Corporation, 171; and economic co-
   operation, 109, 123, 177; electrical
   engineering industry, 85; meat
   production, 86; mechanical engineering in, 84, 85; natural gas in,
   77; petro-chemical industry, 80;
   rubber manufacture, 89; textile
   industry, 89; transport equipment
   industry, 86; transport in, 149, 150
Canada, 70
Capital formation, 113–25; level of
   investment, 115; ICOR, 115. *See
   also* Economic development
Cash, W. C., 134
Central African Republic, 75, 140,
   148; copper production, 3, 71; and
   economic co-operation, 177; lack
   of industrialization, 24; mineral
   surveys, 137; textile industry, 89;
   transport in, 149; and UDEAC,
   123